lonely 🌐 planet

Don't Hike Naked in Switzerland

lonely planet

Don't Hike Naked in Switzerland

and 101 Other Travel Etiquette Tips

Patrick Kinsella

INTRODUCTION 7
HOW TO USE THIS BOOK 10

Public Transportation

13

Lodging

33

Talking to Strangers

51

Dining & Drinking

71

Visiting Local Sites

91

Shopping

113

CONCLUSION 131
INDEX 135

Introduction

TRAVELING, IF YOU'RE DOING IT PROPERLY, often involves passing through the departure gates of your comfort zone and arriving somewhere new. No one knows how to behave perfectly in every single scenario when exploring foreign soil and encountering new cultures, and committing an occasional faux pas is an inevitable part of the experience. As English poet Alexander Pope opined: 'To err is human'. (Although Pope probably didn't pen that line after inadvertently making an offensive hand gesture in front of a sacred site while wearing a crop top, so don't get too comfortable with your poor choices).

The world is a fiendishly and fabulously complex and unpredictable place. Something that's considered heinously rude in one region or country – like loudly and proudly belching after a meal – can be perfectly acceptable, even encouraged, in another. This book is intended to help you steer clear of the worst cultural clangers as you navigate the globe. Because while erring is (definitely) human, to be clued-in and culturally considerate when you're a guest in a country is to be cool.

This isn't intended to be a preachy tome or an atlas of sanctimony, but no one wants an embarrassing international incident to be the most vivid memory of their overseas trip. No one wants to offend their

Traveling, if you're doing it properly, often involves passing through the departure gates of your comfort zone and arriving somewhere new.

hosts, and travelers who make an effort to observe and respect local customs make more friends and have a much richer experience than those who stomp around with no regard for their surroundings. If that's not enough to sway you, in some circumstances, riding roughshod over local moral codes or ignoring cultural restrictions – even if you're just acting like you do at home – can land you in serious trouble with the law (up to and including receiving big fines and stints in a jail cell). So whether you agree with the restrictions or not, it's worth knowing about them so you can make an informed decision about whether you want to visit a certain destination, and then be aware of how to act whilst there – because extending a traveling experience via a stint in the local slammer isn't on anyone's wish list.

Some cities around the world have become so sick of rude tourists that they've begun taking action to discourage visitors. The reasons behind this vary from place to place, but overall are pretty complex – like locals having nowhere to live because of an explosion of Airbnbs – but often it's simply because tourists, especially those in large groups, have been behaving breathtakingly badly.

And why am I the right person to be dishing out advice on travel etiquette? Well, this is one area where it's a good idea to learn from other people's mistakes, and I've made a bunch of them over the three-and-a-bit decades I've been stumbling and blundering around the planet, exploring countries as diverse as **Moldova**, **Malaysia** and **Malawi**, and putting my foot in my mouth everywhere from the **Yukon** to **Tierra del Fuego**. While I never intend to insult or offend, I happen to be pathologically clumsy, primarily left-handed and all-too-often childishly excited, making me a veteran faux-pas collector. (Sorry, fellow southpaws, but the International Etiquette

Police hate us every bit as much as the person who invented scissors, and just eating with your left hand can ruffle feathers in some places.) Now I'm here to help you avoid some of the mistakes I've made personally, and warn against gaffes I've witnessed other hapless travelers commit (usually resulting in much hilarity; other times to a half-stunned, half-seething silence).

But if you take away nothing else, I hope this book brings some food for thought when meeting international travelers in your own backyard. As clueless or jerkish as an out-of-towner might seem in the moment, they're probably just blissfully unaware of the laws and unwritten social norms that govern where you live – like when I spent a week hitchhiking in **East Africa** before someone helpfully told me that sticking your thumb up there is like sticking up your middle finger (amazingly, friendly locals still stopped for me, despite the fact I was flipping them the bird). So, cut your fellow travelers some slack and remember the second part of that Alexander Pope truthbomb: 'To err is human; to forgive, divine.'

HOW TO USE THIS BOOK

In the following chapters we have taken each part of the typical travel experience – from using transport systems and finding somewhere to stay and eat, through to negotiating the dos and definitely don'ts of meeting and greeting local people without triggering an international incident – and supplied some advice. This guidance is seasoned with cautionary tales and pointers about specific fumbles, bumbles and blunders you ought really to avoid, as well as a few cautionary tales.

Planet Earth is a pretty big place, though, and I don't know exactly where you are heading. I can't predict every misstep and mistake you might make while on the road – so you will obviously need to do further research. Visit the Lonely Planet website for more destination-specific information about wherever you're headed.

For now, cover your shoulders (more places are prudish about flashing flesh than you could ever guess, and this applies to men and women), mind your manners and we'll set off. Just don't hike naked or flush the toilet after 10pm in **Switzerland**, cut up your spaghetti with scissors in **Italy**, take a selfie with a Buddha statue in **Sri Lanka**, or stick your thumb up at people in **East Africa** or **Greece**.

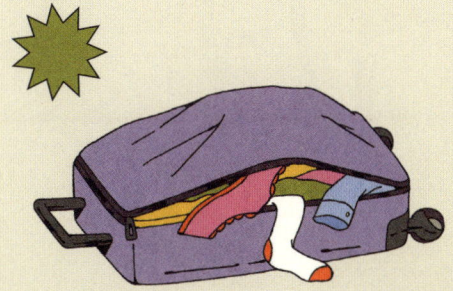

CHAPTER ONE

PLANES, TRAINS & BUSES

PUBLIC TRANSPORTATION

Regardless of whether it has wheels 🚌 or wings, sharing a narrow, fast-moving metal tube with a hundred strangers is an awkward 🧍‍♂️🧍 situation at the best of times — the only way to make it bearable is to avoid being a jerk 😠 to the people around you. I promise it's not that hard. 💥

IN THIS CHAPTER we will provide a guide on how to share mobile public spaces – planes, trains and automobiles – with complete strangers in a way that will help you avoid everything from mild social discomfort and outright hostility to international incidents and forced landings.

Deciphering the quirks and intricacies of a foreign transport network can be mind-melting, but public transportation is an essential part of the traveling experience. You will meet a much broader spectrum of society using trains, trams, subways, boats and buses than you'll ever encounter in a bar, cafe, restaurant or museum, and sharing the thrills and frustrations of everyday travel experiences with ordinary residents is like looking through a window into the un-tidied-up reality of a destination.

Stations, decks and carriages are the kinds of places where spontaneous conversations break out between strangers – especially when things go a bit awry – and this is where serendipity can lead to memorable encounters and impromptu adventures that might transform your trip, or even your life. It's also the second cheapest way to get around after walking.

On the Plane

Unless you're loaded and can afford the plusher seats, flying cattle class is a pretty woeful way to travel. However, being trapped in an air-conditioned tube with hundreds of germ-ridden strangers, all as bored and strung-out as you are for hours on end is an experience most people endure rather than enjoy. And it can be made a whole lot worse by travelers who don't give a crap about the comfort of those around them.

It's not the frazzled families with upset infants that are the problem (those poor parents are suffering more than anyone), it's the adult fly-babies who throw tantrums when they don't get their way and ruin the flight for everyone. The following tips will make sure you aren't that guy everyone wishes would be escorted off the plane pre-takeoff.

A RIGHT CARRY-ON

Most airlines are pretty stringent with their luggage allowances, but there's always someone who manages to take up so much space in the overhead lockers that everyone else has to store their bag ten rows behind their seat. Do you really need enough stuff to survive on a desert island for a month in the event of a crash? You're going to be the first person your fellow passengers eat anyway...

ONE FOR THE ROAD

Airports are one of those rare places you see perfectly normal-looking people sinking beers at breakfast time, without anyone raising an eyebrow. But while pre-holiday pints are a nice novelty, no one wants to sit near a party of obnoxious drunk dudes for hours in the air, nor to have the pie-eyed person in the next seat fall asleep and dribble on them the minute the flight takes off. Even if liquid libations are a big part of your vacation plan, go easy during the journey and save the serious sessions for when you get to your destination.

And while we're at it, holding up the flight by being late to board because you're squeezing in one last drink at the airport bar is another way to earn the ire of everyone else. Feel the heat of those stink-eye stares as you do the wobbly walk of shame along the aisle – you deserve them.

SEAT POLITICS

Reclining your seat to the full extent the minute the seat-belt light goes off, and staying stubbornly supine even when meals are being served, is a cardinal sin. Everyone wants to arrive as fresh as they can, and getting some shut-eye on a long-haul trip is more than reasonable, but you don't need to be horizontal for the entirety of the flight. (And there is a special place waiting in the arrival hall of hell for people who recline during short flights.) Just be reasonable and do unto the traveler sat behind you as you would have the person positioned in front do unto you. Repeatedly kneeing the back of the seat in front of you, commandeering both armrests, draping your Rapunzel-like locks over back of the seat, or poking the TV screen with Bruce Lee–levels of force is also to be avoided.

AISLE STRETCHING

No one wants deep-vein thrombosis as a souvenir from their trip, so it's a good idea to do a few stretches during the flight. However, try not to contort yourself into positions that result in fellow travelers getting a faceful of your butt.

On the Train

TRAVEL ETIQUETTE TIPS

Train travel is, by popular consensus, a wonderful way to get around. During most long-distance journeys you will have enough room to stretch your legs, look out the window and doze off to the rat-a-tat rhythm of the train rolling over the rails. It doesn't take too much, though, for this idyll to be impacted by inconsiderate behavior. Don't be that person who derails the experience for everyone by treating the train like your personal stretch limo.

WHAT TO DO WITH YOUR LUGGAGE

The amount of luggage you haul around determines the kind of traveler you are (sorry, I don't make the rules). From the backpacker trying to squeeze their way through a crowded carriage with all the grace and spatial awareness of a drunk tortoise, to the luxury traveler with an endless ensemble of monogrammed cases, what you take with you is directly proportional to the amount of space you believe you're entitled to take up (and how little you anticipate others will need by comparison).

Regardless of how full-to-bursting your backpack or suitcase is, it doesn't deserve its own seat, especially if the train is busy. Store bags in the overhead luggage racks, between the seats, or in the larger spaces at the end of carriages. If you have to, park your ass on your pack and let someone local have a seat, especially when you're only

TOP TIP

In **Spain**, you can take a ferret on a train, but it will cost you €10 (per ferret). Since 2023, Spanish public train operator Renfe has permitted pets (including dogs, cats, ferrets, guinea pigs, hamsters and rabbits under 10kg/22lb) to be taken on all high-speed routes, for a fee.

going a couple of stops – you'll be an ambassador for us all.

EATING AND DRINKING

One of the delights of train travel is tucking into a picnic while watching the world whizz past the window, or enjoying a drink while someone else does the serious business of driving. Not all foodstuffs are fantastic for consumption in a shared carriage, though, and some extremely aromatic items might elicit more irritation than envy. Eating is never a spectator sport, and no one wants to be sat next to a stranger munching endless egg-and-onion sandwiches, or peeling a piece of fruit that squirts of juice all over the place – so be mindful of this when planning your packed snacks.

DON'T GET HANGRY

SMART TRANSIT SNACKING

Feeding your face on public transport can be a cultural faux pas in many countries, like **Hong Kong** and **Japan**. In **Malaysia**, **Thailand** and **Singapore**, even *carrying* a durian fruit on trains (or buses) is strictly prohibited, let alone trying to eat it. In **Korea** it is considered rude to eat in front of people who are not themselves eating, and this counts whether you're on a bus, train or ferry.

Contrastingly, during long train trips in **India** you're likely to encounter families and friends tucking into massive meals, and they may offer you some food. It would be rude not to accept such a lovely gesture, and you can always reciprocate by sharing some of your own provisions (unless it's a questionable, bottom-of-your-bag snack that smells like an active ingredient made in a prison distillery).

A HIERARCHY OF NEEDS
WHAT TO TAKE ON PUBLIC TRANSIT

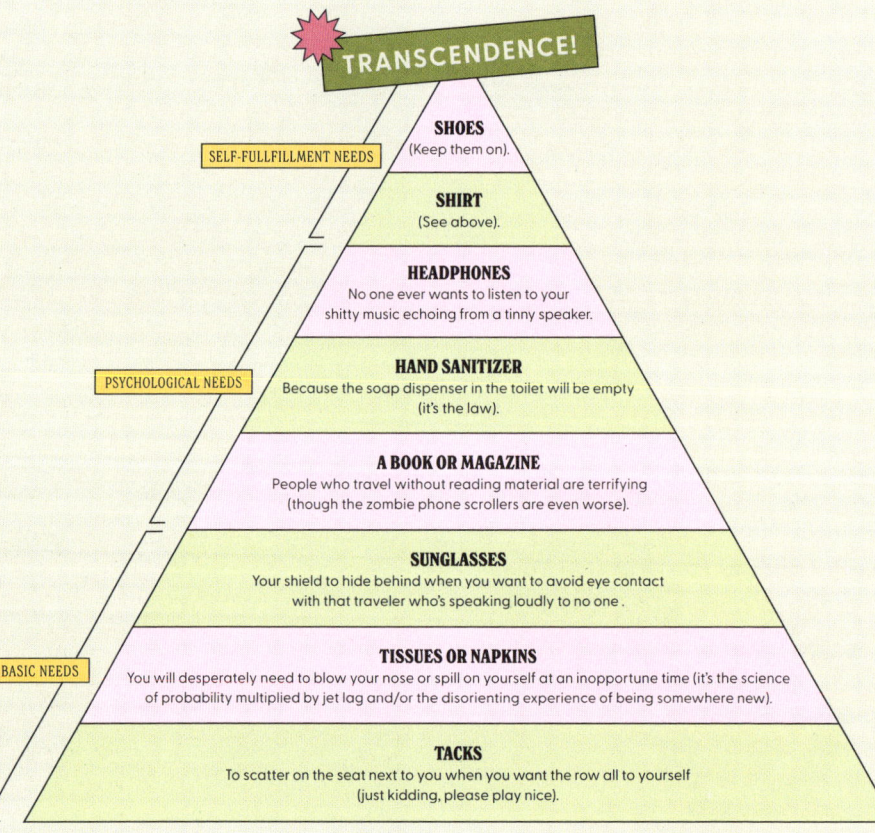

TRANSCENDENCE!

SELF-FULLFILLMENT NEEDS

SHOES
(Keep them on).

SHIRT
(See above).

HEADPHONES
No one ever wants to listen to your shitty music echoing from a tinny speaker.

PSYCHOLOGICAL NEEDS

HAND SANITIZER
Because the soap dispenser in the toilet will be empty (it's the law).

A BOOK OR MAGAZINE
People who travel without reading material are terrifying (though the zombie phone scrollers are even worse).

SUNGLASSES
Your shield to hide behind when you want to avoid eye contact with that traveler who's speaking loudly to no one.

BASIC NEEDS

TISSUES OR NAPKINS
You will desperately need to blow your nose or spill on yourself at an inopportune time (it's the science of probability multiplied by jet lag and/or the disorienting experience of being somewhere new).

TACKS
To scatter on the seat next to you when you want the row all to yourself (just kidding, please play nice).

On the Subway

Urban underground, light-rail and tram services are an excellent way to get around a new city, and they often have their own sets of rules. In bigger cities, there's always a chance you'll encounter someone local breaking all the rules of civil decency by doing something heinous like trimming their toenails or dowsing themselves and everyone around them in perfume, but for the most part everyone just wants to get where they're going with minimal hassle.

Whether you're traveling on the Subway, Tube, Metro, U-Bahn, DART or another system, it's a good idea to familiarize yourself with the local customs and find out what is really frowned upon, because this can differ wildly between destinations. In a recent poll in **Brazil**, locals described the number-one inconsiderate behavior on buses and trains as 'sexual activity', whereas travelers in **Chile**, the **United States**, the **UK** and **Canada** were far more wound up by loud music.

But no matter where you are, talking loudly on a phone, flapping your lips off about what a dump such-and-such a place is, while sprawling over a whole row of seats with your shoes off, is a good way to get everyone within ear- or eyeshot to hate you (and, by association, the rest of the people in your country of origin).

TOP TIP
In **Japan**, despite deference to older people being a cornerstone of the culture, it can be considered extremely rude to presume someone is 'elderly' by offering them your seat. Here, if someone feels they are sufficiently advanced in years to deserve a seat more than others, they will likely tell you directly, especially if you're occupying a seat dedicated to those with greater needs.

But the number one rule of navigating public transit in any country— always let people get off before barging on.

PRIORITY SEATS

In many urban areas it is good manners to give up your seat on a busy train (or bus) so someone elderly, disabled, or pregnant can sit down. However, in some counties this concept can be a bit of a minefield to negotiate. Look out for priority seats, set aside for people who need them the most (usually these are indicated by illustrations), and keep your butt well away from them when the carriage or car is busy.

MAKING POLITE EYE CONTACT

Have you ever stared into space, contemplating the meaning of life and wishing you could astral-project out of an overheated subway car, only to realize you've been staring into the eyes of the (increasingly) nervous stranger across from you? For a while, around 2014, it was common to see stickers on the **London** Underground warning: 'No eye contact. Penalty £200.'

It was, of course, a joke. Or was it? Well yes, the stickers were fake (made by some guerilla comedian with an eye for social commentary), and the fine obviously didn't exist. But no one was

making much eye contact with each other on the Tube then, and they're not now either.

For once, we're going to suggest bucking this unspoken rule and engaging with people. Sure, there are plenty of commuters who would prefer to be in a bubble, and they will probably make that very clear with their body language. Don't persist in pestering people who are clearly transmitting those 'don't bother me' vibes – if you want to play at getting a taciturn stranger to acknowledge your existence, try chatting up one of the King's Life Guard outside **London**'s Buckingham Palace and see where that gets you. But outside of rush hour, public transport in big cities is typically full of fellow travelers, out-of-towners or leisure-minded locals, many of whom are also lost or confused, and may secretly be hoping that a decent human being such as yourself will engage them in pleasant conversation.

Every situation is different and places vary enormously in terms of how strangers interact with one another, but sharing a bus or a train carriage instantly gives you a common denominator, and it often doesn't take too much to get a conversation started. What's the worst that can happen? (Disclaimer: we're not accepting any liability for this going horribly wrong if you misjudge the situation and choose to make lighthearted small talk with the person snarling at their own reflection in the window.)

TOP TIP

Pregnant women in some countries and cities will wear a pin or badge, so strangers don't have to risk making an embarrassingly incorrect judgement call. In **London** you see 'Baby on Board' badges, while in **Japan**, expectant mothers wear a 'maternity mark' (showing an image of a mom and baby) and in **South Korea** pink pregnancy badges can be collected at subway stations – but don't try wearing one unless you are with child (especially you, fellas): they do ask for documentation as proof.

ICEBREAKERS

HOW TO START A CONVERSATION ON THE TRAIN

* Get into a face-pulling competition with a child in a nearby seat (just be sure to make it goofy...not creepy).

* Ask someone where you should get off in order to see a popular local site or attraction.

* Inquire about the correct pronunciation of a place.

* If the person you're sat next to is reading a book, ask if they're enjoying it*, or recommend it. (*Unless said book is *Mein Kampf*, in which case, maybe move away...quickly.)

* Pay someone an innocuous compliment (not a sleazy one, obviously...). Complimenting somebody's band T-shirt can be a great conversation starter, but don't take it as an opportunity to test their music trivia. Being able to name the first three Ramones' albums might make you feel superior, but it's not a good way to make friends.

Taking the Bus

Traveling by bus isn't quite as easy or quick as riding the rails between stations, but it's usually very cheap and you get to see a whole lot more of the city or country you're exploring en route to your planned destination. Many of the same rules mentioned for trains and subways apply here too (if you've already forgotten or aren't paying attention – RUDE – flip back to p. 18 for a refresher). You will, however, be in much closer proximity to your driver, so why not give them a 'hello' when you get on and a 'thanks!' when you get off? Double points for doing this in the local lingo. Don't go bending their ear during the journey, though, asking distracting questions and yabbering on – especially if you're somewhere like the Yungas Road in **Bolivia**, which isn't known as 'Death Road' for nothing.

THIS IS MY STOP!

Although buses bumble along ordinary streets and come to a halt regularly at traffic lights and road junctions, they usually only let people out at designated stops – don't go screaming at the driver to let you off at random intervals just because you need to pee. (Though on longer, cross-country journeys, it's perfectly reasonable to ask when there will be a toilet break.) Most urban buses will have a button to press or cord to pull that lets the driver know you want to get out at the next stop, so you don't need to yell from the back seat. If you have no idea where you should disembark in order to reach a specific place, just politely ask the driver when you board – they'll usually give you a holler when it's time to get off.

TOUR BUSES

You may find yourself taking a guided minibus tour to a local attraction with a posse of other tourists. This is a great way to see neighboring towns and villages, visit several regional highlights, or possibly explore some local vineyards or bazaars. Usually, though, the itineraries for these types of trips are quite tight, with designated drop-off and pick-up times for each port of call – don't be that person who shatters the whole day's schedule because you spent four hours bartering over a rug in the souk or sampling an eighth glass of Chenin Blanc. This isn't to say you shouldn't make the experience your own, but if you get lost in a neighborhood you were cautioned not to go to, and have to be rescued by the tour guide, expect your bus buddies to have some opinions about it on the journey back.

JAYWALKING

(DO NOT) WALK THIS WAY

Even walking can be problematic on your travels. Jaywalking (going from one side of the road to the other without using a pedestrian crossing) is a criminal act in some countries and territories, including many states in **the USA** – something that often comes as a shock to people visiting from countries where adults are allowed to decide when it's safe to cross the road. In **South Korea** you can get a stiff fine for jaywalking, and in **Singapore** the offence can even lead to a three-month jail term if you're putting others in harm. A number of countries, including **France** and **Ireland**, also have laws prohibiting crossing roads if you're within a certain distance of a proper pedestrian crossing (but these are widely ignored by virtually everyone).

TRAVEL ETIQUETTE TIPS

Don't persist in pest(ering?) clearly transmitting (')(leave?) me' vibes—if you wa(nt) a taciturn stranger your existence, try c(hecking?) King's Life Guard o(ut?) Palace and see wher(e)

ring people who are
hose 'don't bother
t to play at getting
o acknowledge
atting up one of the
side Buckingham
that gets you. ✸

PUBLIC TRANSPORTATION

27

Taxis

If you can afford it, taking a taxi or car service makes traveling around easy and hassle-free, but there are often unspoken (and occasionally shouted) rules about how to go about hailing one. Don't stride into the street, raise your arm and expect a cab to appear at your feet like a magic carpet, or screech to a halt like a dog being called to heel – despite what you've seen in the movies, it doesn't work like this and such behavior might get you a one-way ride to nowhere.

In most big cities, cabs can be hailed from the curb (usually a light on the roof of the vehicle will indicate the car is accepting passengers), but typically you will need to find a designated taxi rank and wait in the queue like everyone else. When hailing a taxi from the street, *do* make eye contact with the driver and wait for them to acknowledge you; *do not* just bawl 'TAXI!' at the top of your voice, side-eye any rival cab-catchers and sprint to get hold of the door handle first. Unless your partner is on the verge of giving birth (and even then), this is the quickest way to signal that you're a Stage 5 Cautionary Tale.

WHERE TO SIT IN A TAXI

In **Australia**, if you're traveling on your own in a cab and you *don't* sit next to the driver, he or she will think you're completely up yourself. It's also the expected behavior in much of **Europe**. Try riding shotgun in **Britain** or the **US**, however, and the driver will look at you as if you've just set up camp in their living room, stolen the TV remote and drunk their last beer. In fact, the designer of **London**'s famous black cabs removed the front seat alto-

gether, to avoid any chance of the drivers having their personal space invaded.

MAKING FRIENDS

Even though chatty cabbies are being replaced with screens or silence, no matter where in the world you are (or what part of the car you're sitting in), some cabbies still love to talk, and a conversation with your driver can give you an interesting insight into the place you're visiting. They (should) know the city inside and out, and often offer a colorful opinion on everything from tourist traps to local politics. Take the opportunity to rap with a real resident, just bear in mind that taxi drivers often see the worst behavior imaginable from both visitors and locals, so their views can be formed accordingly.

TIPPING

Most taxi drivers will appreciate a tip – even just rounding up the fare or chucking in an extra 10% is appropriate in places like the **United Kingdom**, **Ireland** and across most of **Europe** (except **Scandinavia**, where it's really not expected). In some countries, however – such as **Iceland**, **Singapore**, **Japan** and **South Korea** – offering a driver a gratuity for a service you're already paying for can cause confusion, embarrassment or even offense.

TOP TIP

There are lots of "unofficial" taxi companies that offer their services at airports or major tourist hotspots with the hopes of scamming unsuspecting newcomers. Don't get taken for a ride—only accept lifts from marked cars or companies you can verify. Airports, hotels, and major cultural centers will likely be able to offer trustworthy recommendations.

Car Rental

Hiring some wheels enables you to properly explore a region or island with complete independence. Try not to trash the vehicle, though, because that's not just rude – it wrecks the rep of all travelers, and raises prices. You probably wouldn't attempt to eat a triple-scoop ice cream cone while driving your SUV at home, so don't do it while steering your rented Jeep during your vacation.

If you're having trouble remembering what side of the road to drive on, stick something really obvious on the dash to remind you – because there's nothing that upsets locals and ruins a travel experience more than having a head-on collision.

✶ HELPFUL ✶
DOS AND DON'TS

ON PLANES, TRAINS & BUSES

DO take your litter with you, or find a bin – people who stick chewing gum on the undersides of tables, or leave the seat looking like a crime scene are savages

DON'T be that person who instantly gets up the second a plane lands, and stands with their butt in your face for the next 20 minutes

DO pack sensibly, so you don't require an entire carriage for your luggage like some self-entitled royal entourage

DON'T treat fare evasion as a sport, then pull the wide-eyed hapless tourist routine when you get collared

DO try and wait until you're somewhere a little more discreet before physically expressing your adoration for your traveling partner

DON'T play loud music or games without headphones (they're a great invention)

DO consider the passenger behind you before putting your seat down

DON'T eat stinky or overly sticky food

DO keep your cool when collecting your luggage – standing right beside the carousel and shoulder barging everyone else out the way won't make your bags arrive any quicker

DON'T sit in the window seat and then pull the blind down so no one can look out

DON'T take up empty seats with your feet or bags, especially when it's busy

PUBLIC TRANSPORTATION

CHAPTER TWO

HOTELS, HOSTELS & B&BS

LODGING

Traveling means sleeping in 🛏 different places, and when you stay anywhere that isn't your own sweet home, 🏢 the floor of the foyer, dining area, corridor or common room is often scattered with metaphorical banana skins, just waiting for you to slip 🍌 on and land with one foot in your mouth. ✴

EVERY COUNTRY, REGION AND CITY has its little (and not so little) local quirks when it comes to homestays and boutique accommodation. A situation where you are essentially sleeping in someone's home (either because they have invited you, or because you're paying for the privilege) presents the perfect opportunity to learn about and observe the customs and manners practiced in the country. Start by doing some research, and then follow the lead set by your hosts and any fellow guests with local experience and knowledge. This is a wonderful way to learn about authentic everyday life in a foreign country – and your host won't expect you to be completely clued in on everything prior to arrival, so don't spend the whole time walking on eggshells (just try and avoid clumsily stamping on cultural sensitivities).

Here we offer some salient advice on how not to offend your local hosts or make a total jerk of yourself when overnighting in hotels, hostels, homestays, guesthouses, inns and B&Bs.

Hotels

Hotels vary enormously according to where they are, the tariff charged and the number of stars twinkling beside their name, but no matter how much you're shelling out for your room, there are good and very bad ways to behave when you're staying in one. For starters, you're not Keith Moon, so getting blazed on booze and drugs and throwing the TV set through the window is definitely out (that kind of carry on is so passé, and modern flat-screen TVs are really hard to get off the wall anyway). But there's more to being a decent hotel guest than resisting the temptation to trash your room and then go down for breakfast sans pants.

BOOKING AND CHECKING IN

When making a booking, let the hotel know what time you're likely to arrive and generally they will try and work with you – turning up early and being rude to staff because your room isn't ready gets you nowhere fast. When you arrive, be friendly from the get-go. You might even score an upgrade or a room with a better view.

AMENITIES

'Reserving' recliners around the hotel swimming pool by draping your towel or leaving belongings on them before disappearing for hours is a cheap trick, and you deserve all those stink-eye stares if you indulge in such skullduggery. In **Spain** – where vicious sunbed wars have erupted between territorial tourists attempting to hog the hot spots around the pool and on the resort's beachfront – hotels have implemented strict bans on such behavior and local police will even issue fines and confiscate personal property to flagrant offenders. If these kinds of shenanigans are occurring around you, take it as a prompt to get out and find some local swimming spots – it will be far more interesting and you won't have to share oxygen with selfish asses.

HELPING YOURSELF

It can be a hard habit to kick after spending time backpacking and dirtbagging around the world (and we've all taken extra bottles of shower gel, shampoo and soap when packing up to leave), but taking everything that's not nailed down every time you go near a hotel pushes the prices up for everyone; and lifting linen can really land you in hot water. Some hotel chains in the **USA** use RFID tags in their towels, so they can be traced. But more than likely – if you're lucky enough to spend a night at a hotel with monogrammed robes worth stashing – anything you thought you were clever enough to steal will still wind up on

your bill. And bear in mind, too, that in places such as **Japan** and **Nigeria**, light-fingered hotel guests have been arrested for stealing things like towels, robes and ashtrays.

ROOM SERVICE

Treat room service as a last resort – it's usually overpriced, makes your room stink, creates a mess for housekeepers and channels more cash into the coffers of big companies, instead of local businesses. Ask the concierge for a recommendation for a good local restaurant or, better still, go explore to see what culinary treasures you can find. If you do end up having food in your room, don't eat saucy meals on the bed and leave a mess that resembles a scene from a Tarantino movie for the staff to deal with.

TOP TIP

If you miss last orders at the local restaurants, try a late night takeaway, but don't attempt to bring that filthy burger back to your room unless you're prepared for guests three floors away to complain to about the smell.

TRAVEL ETIQUETTE TIPS

'Reserving' recliners
swimming pool by d
leaving belongings
appearing for hours
you deserve all thos
you indulge in such

around the hotel
aping your towel or
 them before dis-
is a cheap trick, and
stink-eye stares if
kullduggery.

PAYMENT AND TIPPING

Even in countries where tipping isn't the norm, like **Australia**, **New Zealand/Aotearoa**, **Britain** and **Ireland**, and across much of **Europe** hotel porters and housekeepers will appreciate a small gratuity for good service, but don't flash your cash left, right and center, because this can cause confusion and/or discomfort. Minimum-wage laws are in place in these countries so staff are not reliant on tips, and a service charge is often included in bills. If you want to leave a token of appreciation and be sure it ends up in the right pocket, give big coins or small notes directly to the person you want to thank.

Hotel workers in **Scandinavia** and **Iceland** may seem shocked to receive a tip – it's really not the norm in these locations, and with the sky-high prices, you're better off keeping your dough for dining out and enjoying various experiences.

In the **United States**, however, repeatedly forgetting to tip the people hauling your luggage around and changing your sheets, or the concierge directing you towards all the best places, will likely result in a quick reduction of enthusiasm and helpfulness; likewise across **Central and South America**. In **Canada**, tips are also expected, but some hotels will add a service charge and discourage tipping of individuals (this is usually made clear in the T&Cs – but even in that case, leaving a tip won't cause offense).

Tips are expected and highly appreciated in hotels across **Africa** and the **Caribbean**, where the concierge will ensure you get good service and advice if you cross their palm with silver (probably best to stick to local currency, or US dollars though).

Tipping in **Asia** isn't quite as straightforward. In some places, such as **India**, hotel staff are extremely poorly paid and offering even a modest tip (by most travelers' standards) can make a big difference. Tips are not expected from hotel guests in **China**; across most of **Southeast Asia** (including **Cambodia**, **Indonesia**, **Malaysia**, the **Philippines**, **Singapore**, **Thailand** and **Vietnam**), a service charge is usually included in the bill you get when checking out, but small thank-you gestures given directly to staff won't cause offense.

In **Japan**, however, openly tipping can cause acute embarrassment to the recipient because it's not expected and can appear crass. If you're staying in a traditional *ryokan* (inn), and you really want to leave a gesture of appreciation, put a modest amount in an envelope and place it somewhere obvious with a little thank-you note. (Or come prepared and bring a thoughtful gift from your home country: something small and traditional, such as food or drink; or cute, like a cuddly toy representing a native animal, if your host has children.)

TOP TIP

In some **Muslim countries** it's technically illegal for unmarried couples to share double hotel rooms. This law is largely overlooked, especially in glitzy establishments, but to avoid any scenes it's worth maintaining a facade. You don't need to go over the top and start scowling and yelling at one another, but if the person checking you in asks whether you're married, answer sensibly. Sadly, same-sex relationships are also illegal in these countries, and in many others. And no matter what gender you are, or what kind of relationship you're in, subtlety is crucial when traveling with your partner in these places. In practice, very few people care what you do behind closed doors, but public displays of affection are massively disapproved of.

B&Bs

TRAVEL ETIQUETTE TIPS

Bed-and-breakfast accommodations can be found in many countries, but the concept was born in **Britain**, and is especially common in **England**, **Scotland**, **Wales** and across **Ireland**. These small, family-owned establishments remain an essential experience for the anecdote-collecting traveler. Traditionally, a stay in a B&B is a more intimate experience than a typical hotel. Guests are provided with a room in someone's house (usually a historic home or farmhouse), with the option of joining other guests in a communal dining room each morning to eat half your body weight in fried farmyard produce.

IMPORTANT B&B REMINDERS

※ This is not a hotel or hostel, where you can come and go at all hours of the night as you please, so don't be surprised if the host gives you a curfew and a hard stare when handing over the keys. Even if they don't, this is not the best place to stay if you're planning on clubbing until 4am. ※ You will almost certainly be sharing a dining room, and very often a table, with other guests for breakfast – so don't swan in wearing just your undies and a halo of bed-hair. ※ Don't expect an evening meal (or lunch). These places are known as 'Bed and Breakfasts' for a reason. (Occasionally a host will offer more, but don't rely on it.)

A MAZE

MAKE YOUR WAY BACK HOME

Uh oh, you had too much wine and lost your way! Grab a pen and see if you can find your way back to your hotel without getting stuck.

Airbnb

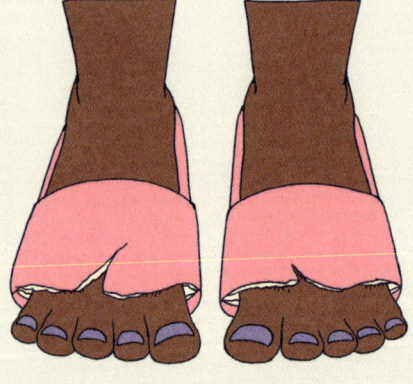

Many entrepreneurial types have taken the quaint concept of renting rooms to visitors in an otherwise ordinary house and super-sized it into the controversial colossus that is Airbnb. Now anyone can be a host, and people take creative photos of everything from their entire castle to their broom cupboard or a cave at the bottom of the garden, and hawk it as idyllic holiday accommodation – often to the abject horror of their neighbors.

A large proportion of Airbnbs are operated by private landlords who run their buy-to-let properties as tourist-catering properties, making the original premise of people renting out their homes a distant memory. Whether you think this is the best thing to happen to travelers since budget flights took off, or the beginning of the end for civilization as we know it, Airbnb is here to stay for the foreseeable future (although it's technically illegal to operate an Airbnb in **Thailand**, and there are very tight restrictions on it in many countries and cities, from **Japan** and **Barcelona** to **Jersey City** and **Boston**). If you're someone who gives a hoot about others, and ethics are as equally important to you as new experiences, do your research first; if you're visiting a location with an acute housing problem, explore alternative accommodation options (such as real B&Bs, homestays or Fairbnb, which directs a percentage of bookings to social projects in the local area).

If you do opt for an Airbnb, the golden rule is to be respectful towards the people living their ordinary lives around you. Having a birthday gathering in a remote cliff-top tower is one thing; renting a property in a residential area and throwing a 48-hour foam party for all your mates is a gigantic jerk move.

TOP TIP

Across much of **Asia** – in countries including **Japan**, **China** and **India** – it's the height of bad manners to enter someone's house with your outdoor shoes on.

SLIPPER ETIQUETTE

START ON THE RIGHT FOOT

In places where it's customary to remove outdoor shoes, your hosts will often have some slippers on hand (or foot) for guests to use, but be sure to wear good, clean socks – rocking up with your toes poking through holes, or stank feet, would be mortifying for all involved. If you're traveling extensively in these places, and you're lucky enough to be visiting people in their homes, it's worth packing your own indoor footwear (especially if you have big flippers and don't want to feel like one of Cinderella's ugly stepsisters).

Rules around slippers are particularly strict in **Japan**, where most houses and many hostels have a dedicated area by the front door called the genkan, where you transition from outdoor to indoor footwear. It doesn't stop there, though, because a second set of slippers must be donned when you use the bathroom. The absolute worst thing you can do is to follow all this protocol, and then forget to change out of your toilet slippers after leaving the bathroom, thus traipsing across the beautiful tatami mats in your loo shoes.

Hostels

Hostels can be wonderful places to meet people from all over the world and learn valuable, on-the-ground information about the city, region or country you're traveling through. But cramming lots of people from all over the globe into a small space can get dicey, and it only takes one bozo for things to turn ugly.

PREVENTING HOSTILE HOSTEL STAYS

This might sound unnervingly similar to the kind of advice someone might give a new cellmate doing their first stint in the joint, but the following tips should help keep things friendly:

✺ No matter what bunk you're in, don't use the ladder as a clothes horse.
✺ If you spark up a sudden romantic relationship, don't pursue it in your shared dorm – get a private room. Seriously, do. ✺ Hostel showers might not be the best, but use them; multiple-occupancy rooms can get funky very quickly if people's personal hygiene starts to slide. ✺ If you're making or taking a phone call, don't do it in the dorm while people are snoozing or reading. ✺ Keep your kit together, don't have it sprawled all over the room (especially if you're leaving early in the morning – in which case get it packed the night before). ✺ Label your food if you're stashing it in the

TOP TIP

Be very careful of randomly pushing the buttons on the remote-control device that drives the high-tech toilets you find in many hotel rooms in **Japan**, especially if you are sitting on the seat at the time. We're not sure what the correct kanji character for 'surprise enema' is, but it's definitely included as a service on some 'conveniences'.

communal kitchen, and keep your hands off other people's sweets and treats, no matter how appealing they look at midnight. ☀ Wash up any pots, pans, cutlery and crockery you have used, straight after you've finished eating. ☀ Be considerate of others and available amenities – that one shonky, fire-hazard power socket in the dorm is not exclusively for you and your dying phone. ☀ Sort out who is using which bunk long before bed time. (A round of rock paper scissors should keep things civilized.) ☀ Make sure you know exactly what bed you're in before you come stumbling into the dorm after the bar has shut (and double-check it's empty before jumping in). ☀ Take a headtorch with a color-beam option

THE LOO-DOWN

TOILET TRAINING

If you're staying somewhere – in a lodging, hostel or hotel – and there's a sign saying you shouldn't flush paper down the toilet, do not assume this doesn't apply to you. Blocking the sewerage system for a whole house, hostel, hotel or street is a great way to make instant enemies. Countries where paper (or anything else, other than the political promises you've specifically gone in there to express) typically can't be flushed include **Brazil**, **China**, **Egypt**, **Greece** and **India**. A bin will be provided. Use it.

In many buildings in **Switzerland**, flushing the toilet after 10pm is – if not actually illegal (as some sites claim) – at least seriously frowned upon. To avoid disturbing other guests or residents, you need to wait until 7am.

Conversely, not flushing a used toilet is an actual criminal offense in **Singapore**, and it can earn you a fine of $1000. (We've never experienced it ourselves, but probably best not to test it).

47

(red, green or blue), so you can find what you're looking for – or take a toilet break – in the middle of the night without flooding the entire dorm in bright white light from your phone.
✺ If you're a light sleeper, bring earplugs and an eye mask so you don't end up raging at the hapless snorer on a nearby bunk. ✺ If you are getting up early to catch a flight, bus or train, put your alarm on vibrate so you don't wake everyone.

TRAVEL ETIQUETTE TIPS

☀ HELPFUL ☀
DOS AND DON'TS
AT HOTELS, HOSTELS & B&BS

DO communicate with your hosts or the hotel/hostel you're staying with – if you're turning up early or late, or have a special request, let them know and they'll usually try and help you out.

DON'T try and sneak 12 people and a dog into a double-occupancy room. It's not comfortable or cool.

DO be nice to the concierge. Obviously you should be polite and respectable to everyone, but life is better if you treat the concierge like a friend (with the understanding that they have many other guests to take care of).

DON'T jabber loudly on your phone in communal areas.

DO wear shoes before coming down for breakfast.

DON'T bring whiffy, greasy food into your room – especially if you're sharing the space with others.

DO use indoor slippers when traveling in Asia.

DON'T leave any surprises (other than a tip) for long-suffering service staff to deal with.

DO pay attention to signage – especially in the toilet.

DON'T steal everything that's not nailed down from your holiday suite.

DO consider other options besides Airbnb when booking accommodation.

LODGING

CHAPTER THREE

HELLOS, THANK YOUS & FAREWELLS

TALKING TO STRANGERS

Meeting new people, especially from cultures and corners of the planet completely different from your own, is one of the reasons we love to wander the world.

STRIKING UP CONVERSATIONS with fellow travelers is typically pretty easy – there are usually ample opportunities to get chatting when you're sharing communal spaces, and most people are open to new encounters when they're on the road. Breaking the ice with *locals*, however, can be harder and more fraught with potential faux pas – not least because you're floundering around on unfamiliar ground, and they're just trying to get on with their everyday lives.

In recent years, some cities – such as **Venice**, **Amsterdam**, **Barcelona**, **Prague**, **Kyoto**, **Edinburgh**, **Dublin** and **Liverpool** – have become so overwhelmed with visitors (and underwhelmed by their behavior) that officials have proposed or imposed tourist taxes, and some residents have even organized demonstrations. If positive interaction with locals is important to you, then try and visit popular places such as these well outside peak periods, and avoid turning up with 63 semi-clad buddies on a boisterous bachelor/bachelorette bash.

No matter where you are, the golden rule is to be open to non-threatening conversations with the people you meet – you'll almost always learn something new about the country or its culture.

Navigating New Languages

Whether it's through idleness, arrogance or anxiety about looking and sounding stupid, English speakers are famously reticent to try new languages, preferring to stick to their own and just turn the volume up. It might be easy to gesture for the bill or signal that you want another beer, but most people will quickly realize that using your hands to convey complex requirements is challenging (try pantomiming to a pharmacist in **Egypt** or **Ecuador** that you've got a severely upset stomach and a long-distance bus to catch, and see what you come up with).

In the era of Duolingo and Google translate, many tourists and travelers (even English speakers) are making more of an effort to learn a few basic

words while they're visiting, (and hopefully engaging in conversations at a normal decibel level). However, sprinkling a few new words into a conversation without understanding the language can be dangerous. Even if the person you're attempting to talk to overlooks the way you've brutally mangled their mother tongue, it's likely you won't catch every word. Depending on the language, your bad pronunciation could be the difference between a happy conversation and an inappropriate F-bomb. Still, running the risk of being misunderstood or left red-faced after dropping a clanger is far better than not bothering to try at all. In most cases, people will genuinely appreciate you making the effort, even if they can't help grinning at the result.

TOP TIP

You might have the best politics according to your circle of friends, but loudly prattling on about the most contentious issues of the day over a breakfast with complete strangers often ends with someone getting their sausage seriously out of joint, and this can be very awkward in mixed company.

RESPECT YOUR ELDERS

AGE BEFORE BEAUTY

In many cultures, when arriving at a location (whether it's a private home, a restaurant table or wherever), it is deemed important to greet the oldest person in the room first, before shaking anyone else's hand (although, if you're meeting strangers, this might involve a scary judgement call as you work out the order of antiquity of those present). You will encounter this in places as far apart as **Oman**, **Malaysia** and **Zimbabwe**, but nowhere is respect for greeting older people given more gravity than in **the Philippines**, where the custom of *mano po* sees young people ask permission to take hold of the hand of an elder and place the back of it on their forehead to show reverence, and to ask for a blessing.

When (and How) to Say Hello

In most languages, 'Hello' is a simple, short word that's easy to say, and doesn't require a complicated response. (Of course there are always exceptions – in **Zulu** it's '*Ngiyakwemukela*'.) Using the local greeting will get your interaction off on the right foot, instantly revealing you've done some research and are happy to dive into the intricacies of the local language and culture.

Almost everywhere it's important to maintain eye contact when saying hello, so the greeting looks sincere. In some cultures, when meeting several people at once, it's expected that you greet people in a certain order, or by using a particular wording, according to age, social status and/or gender. (Even if you have strong feelings about this, deliberately breaking these rules is likely to cause embarrassment as well as offense.)

Such considerations aside, knowing what – if any – physical gestures should be performed with this salutation, and to whom and in which circumstances, is much more complicated and fraught with potential faux pas. Should you shake hands, perform a bow, go in for a hug, start planting kisses on people's cheeks – or avoid all of the above completely?

TAKING THE KISS

In many countries, greetings are accompanied with a kiss on the cheek

TOP TIP
Never, ever tap someone on the head in **Thailand** (and elsewhere in **Asia**), where the head is considered sacred and this action conveys extreme disrespect. Also refrain from sitting on pillows intended for people to lay their heads on.

A CHEEKY KISS CHEAT SHEET

HOW MANY PECKS DO I GET?

Country	Pecks		Country	Pecks
ARGENTINA	♥		MACEDONIA	♥♥♥
BELGIUM	♥♥♥		MONTENEGRO	♥♥♥
BOSNIA	♥♥		NETHERLANDS	♥♥♥
BRAZIL	♥♥(♥) *3 for some regions		PHILIPPINES	♥
CHILE	♥		PERU	♥
COLOMBIA	♥		ROMANIA	♥♥
CROATIA	♥♥		RUSSIA	♥♥♥ + bear hug
EGYPT	♥♥♥♥		SERBIA	♥♥♥
GERMANY	♥♥		SLOVENIA	♥♥♥
GREECE	♥♥		SPAIN	♥♥
HUNGARY	♥♥		SWITZERLAND	♥♥♥
ITALY	♥♥ *start on the left		VENEZUELA	♥♥♥

(or both cheeks). The exact origins of this gesture are lost to the mists of time, but it dates back several millennia, and is often said to have started in Ancient Rome. *Il bacio* (the kiss) certainly remains a very strong tradition in **Italy**. You will encounter *los besos* in **Spain** and *la bise* in **France**, and cheek-kissing happens across much of **Europe**, too, plus in places where the influence of these countries has embedded into local customs and culture, like **Latin America**, and in some **Middle Eastern** countries and parts of **Asia**.

A kiss also means different things in different places. In **Europe** and **Latin America** it typically implies friendship and familiarity, but in the **Middle East** it can denote deference, respect and honor. But, who do you kiss? Just friends and family, or everyone you meet? How many pecks do you go in for, and on which cheek? Without some prior knowledge, the risk of making a mortifying mistake or suffering an undignified collision is pretty high.

In **Italy**, **France** and **Spain**, planting two kisses (one on each cheek) is de rigueur, but in **Belgium** and the **Netherlands** a three-kiss embrace is favored. Most **South American** countries tend to stick with one kiss, but in **Brazil** expect two or three kisses (it varies from region to region). In **Egypt** and elsewhere in the **Middle East**, four kisses on the cheek are common, while in **Afghanistan** up to eight kisses can be exchanged between men greeting one another. In most parts of **Britain**, **Ireland**, the **United States**, **Canada**, **Australia** and **New Zealand/Aotearoa**, however, if you're a tourist greeting a complete stranger, leaning in for one peck on the cheek can come across as pretentious or over-familiar, especially outside of the more bohemian bits of the big cities (unless you're meeting your mom). Your best bet is to take cues from who you're meeting—as long as you're polite, people will give you grace.

In **Latin America** and parts of

Europe, it's quite common for kissing/cheek-brushing to take place even during a first meeting, but elsewhere face-pecks are generally reserved for people you know well. To complicate things further, there are lots of local variations concerning how (or if) you actually land the kiss. In **Italy**, **France** and **Spain** it's common to lightly brush cheeks rather than plant a proper smacker. Elsewhere, including in the **Middle East**, people prefer to perform an air kiss with no physical contact at all, with or without sound effects (this takes some perfecting, if you want to avoid coming across as overly flamboyant). In **Europe** and **Latin America**, women kiss women and men in greeting, and vice versa, and in some places (such as southern **Italy**, **Serbia** and **Argentina**) men also kiss men. Frankly, it's a minefield. Check out the sidebar on p. 59 for more tips on avoiding kissing misfires.

LENDING A HAND

In countries where cheek-kissing isn't common, shaking hands is often expected when meeting new people. Sadly for sinistral globetrotters, strolling up to a stranger and offering your left hand to shake is a big no-no across large swathes of the world. In

SMOOCHING RULES

AVOID THE 'KISS-FIRE'

* Do what's customary with close friends and family, but when it comes to meeting and greeting local people you've just met or don't know very well, follow their lead.

* Refrain from landing your lips on someone's cheek unless they make definite contact with you.

* Kisses or cheek-to-cheek brushes usually start on the right and then swap to the left (if multiple pecks are required) – except in Italy, where *il bacio* starts on the left.

* During the exchange, try not to stand there awkwardly with your body as stiff as a plank – but also don't assume that cheek-kissing should be accompanied by hugging. Take your lead from locals, but if in doubt place your hands gently on the other person's upper arms or shoulders.

many countries across the **Middle East** and **Asia**, including **India**, the left hand is used during toilet duties and is therefore considered unclean. (For the same reason, don't use your left hand to pass food or gifts to people.) One exception is **Kenya**, where it's fine to grasp people's right wrist with your left hand and boom out a big friendly '*Jambo! mambo!*' (Hello! What's up?).

Again, follow the locals' lead, but if you don't want to immediately alienate people when you first meet them with a bad handshake, avoid making it bone-breakingly firm – it's a greeting, not a grappling contest. This is especially important in **China**, **Indonesia**, **South Korea** and **Türkiye**, where an overly aggressive grip is considered very rude. However, neither should you offer a limp hand that feels like a piece of disinterested seaweed – especially in **Russia**, **Australia**, **New Zealand/Aotearoa**, **Britain** and most of **Northern Europe** and **North America**. Don't hang on too long (although expect a lengthier handshake in **Brazil** and **Mexico**; and in **Türkiye**, **Morocco**, across the **Middle East** and **Fiji**, where handshakes can morph into friendly hand-holding). Usually it's best to look the person whose hand you are shaking directly in the eye during the exchange (but not in **China**, where it's considered overly familiar unless you know the person very well). In **Austria**, it's good manners to shake everyone's hand when you enter a room.

In **Zimbabwe** it's traditional to combine a handshake with clapping (after the shake, the first person claps once, and the second person claps twice in response), while in **northern Mozambique** you should clap your hands three times before performing a greeting. When shaking hands in **Botswana**, your thumb should interlock with the thumb of the person you're greeting (in classic bro style), as you clasp their right elbow in your left hand. The Maasai people in **Kenya** and northern **Tanzania** will spit on their hands before shaking as a show of respect – but we don't recommend imitating this one unless you are very sure it's an appropriate scenario.

USING THE FORMAL VS THE INFORMAL

In many places, but especially **Asia**, it's extremely important to be respectful to people who are older than you by fine-tuning your manners and language to show deference. For example, when addressing elders in **China**, etiquette dictates the use of the word *'nin'*, the polite version of 'you' in Mandarin; so if you have done the right thing and learned however to say hello (*'ni hao'*), change that to *'nin hao'* when you are greeting an older Chinese person.

Try chatting to an *ajumma* (older woman) in **Korea** in an overly familiar language, or fail to give way in a queue, and she'll soon let you know all about it (and don't let her hear you call her an *ajumma*, either). It can be hard to work out exactly where the defining lines lie (how much older than you does someone need to be in order to pull rank?), so take your lead from locals, who navigate this gray area with aplomb, and if you're in any doubt, err on the side of caution and use formal terms and language.

HOW TO BOW

In **Japan** and **Korea**, the polite way to acknowledge someone when you meet them is by bowing, a gesture of greeting and respect that is rooted in Confucian philosophy, where respect for elders, hierarchy and social harmony is all important. Inevitably, bowing is not as simple as it sounds, and there are different forms according to your position in life and the age and status of the person you are greeting. Typically, the deeper and longer the bow, the more respect it denotes, but travelers will be forgiven for not knowing all the complexities of the tradition – just make sure to dodge the main pitfalls.

Ensure you maintain a sensible distance from the person you're greeting, to avoid headbutting one another (at which point all attempts to display respect and dignity die). Do not attempt to shake hands while bowing (a classic faux pas committed by then-US president Barack Obama when he met Japanese Emperor Akihito in 2009) – there is a definite risk of a head collision with this approach, but it also conflates two very different greetings. As a rule, your hands should be by your sides when bowing. Also, avoid eye contact: keep

TRAVEL ETIQUETTE TIPS

If positive interacti[on]
is important to you,
popular places such [as]
peak periods, and a[void]
with 63 semi-clad bu[ddies]
bachelor/bachelore[tte]

n with locals
hen try and visit
s these well outside
oid turning up
dies on a boisterous
e bash.

A BOWING GUIDE

ANGLES OF COMMUNICATION

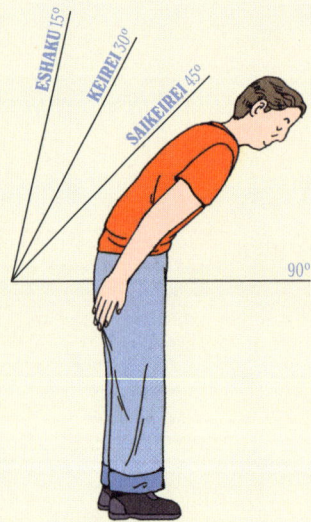
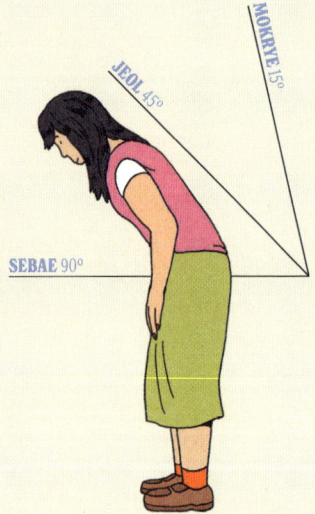

MAIN BOWS OF JAPAN

ESHAKU 15° ANGLE
Used when greeting people of the same age and social status as you.

KEIREI 30° ANGLE
Used to show respect to someone older and/or who occupies a more senior social or professional position.

SAIKEIREI 45° ANGLE
Used to greet a person of great importance (or to apologize for something serious).

MAIN BOWS OF KOREA

MOKRYE 15° ANGLE
Used to greet friends, acquaintances and colleagues, with your hands placed at your sides or in front of you.

JEOL 45° ANGLE
Used to greet people older and more senior than you, involves placing your hands on your thighs. The longer you hold it, the more respect it conveys.

SEBAE 90° ANGLE
Used for meeting royalty, religious leaders and when attending funerals, kneel on both knees with your head to the ground.

your legs and back straight, bend from the waist, lower your head and look at your shoes.

Bowing is traditional in **China** too, but has fallen from fashion in recent years and isn't expected from travelers. Still, the occasional bow might impress your hosts, especially if you do it correctly. Instead of placing your hands by your sides, clasp them together in front of you, observing the 'male left, female right' rule, so men have their left hand on the outside and women have their right hand on the outside (this is reversed at funerals, but let's not get into that...). From the waist, lower your head and look at your shoes.

WAI TO GO

In **Thailand** the traditional way to greet someone is with the *wai*, which involves bringing your hands together, palms facing one another and fingers pointing upwards (as if praying) and doing a slight bow or nod of the head while saying hello or goodbye. It's important to perform the *wai* to the oldest people present first, as a sign of respect; and if the person you are greeting is older and/or occupies a higher social status than you, raise your hands higher (to your forehead) and bow lower.

Similar gestures are used in **Cambodia** (where it's known as the *sampeah*), **Laos** (the *nop*), **Sri Lanka** (*añjali mudrā*) and **Bali**, where it's accompanied by the expression 'Om suastiastu' (peace and greetings from God).

In **India** and **Nepal**, the ubiquitous greeting ritual also involves bringing your hands together as though praying, and saying *'Namaste'*, a Sanskrit word that literally means 'I bow to you', while doing a very shallow bow.

TOP TIP

In most **Asian** countries, elderly people are given the honor of entering or leaving a room first, so hang back if you're young.

Sign Language and Gesture Politics

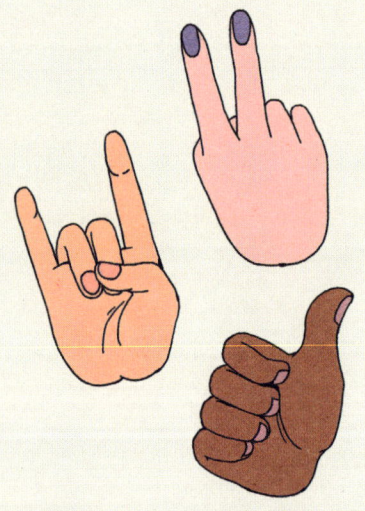

Inadvertently using an inappropriate hand gesture while traveling is one the easiest ways to cause unintended offense. Gestures that are completely innocuous at home can mean something entirely different when you're abroad, so if you're prone to gesticulating, it's worth doing some research. The following gestures are some of the most common offenders:

✺ It's best not to point at all, but doing it using just your index finger is considered very rude in many cultures (this is why flight attendants and Disney theme park characters point with two fingers).

✺ The 'OK' signal (index finger touching thumb) is deemed obscene (denoting the anus) in several places, including **Türkiye, Tunisia, Greece** and **Brazil** (where President Nixon caused a furor when he used this gesture while stepping off a plane in the 1950s). In the **Middle East** it symbolizes the 'evil eye.' It has also become connected to far right groups, and has been declared a symbol of hate in some parts of the **USA**, so be mindful when you use it. ✺ Avoid using the rock'n'roll horns hand gesture (raising your index and little fingers) in

Italy, Spain, Greece and Brazil, where it symbolizes a bull's horns and implies a man's wife is cheating on him. ☀ Giving the thumbs up is the equivalent of flipping the bird in Iran, Greece, Russia, Sardinia and much of West Africa. ☀ Waggling your index finger to suggest someone come towards you is deemed offensive in many Asian countries, where it's used to beckon dogs. In the Philippines it implies you're in serious trouble, and in Singapore this gesture symbolizes death. ☀ In Britain, sticking two fingers up with your palm facing inwards (the reverse of the peace sign) is an insult, which supposedly dates to medieval times, when captured archers would have their index and middle fingers cut off. A (probably apocryphal) story links this gesture to the 1415 Battle of Agincourt, where English archers allegedly taunted French soldiers with it, showing they still had their fingers. ☀ In Greece, extending an open hand with palm pointing outwards and fingers outstretched is known as the *moutza*, and (for reasons that date right back to a humiliating punishment meted out during the Byzantine Empire era) is highly offensive. Be mindful of this when waving at people, because the gestures can easily be confused. ☀ Crossing your index and middle fingers – often

AN OLIVE BRANCH

SAVING FACE WHEN YOU'VE MADE A MISTAKE

Sorry is famously the hardest word to say – especially if you're in **Hawai'i**, where you have to wrap your tongue around the expression *kala mai ia'u* if you need to apologize. Contrition is a virtue, though, and given there's a fairly high likelihood you're going to unintentionally commit some sort of social faux pas while traveling across unfamiliar ground and mixing in cultures that differ from your own, 'sorry' is one of the words you should definitely learn to say in the local language.

In **Japan**, a sincere apology should be accompanied by a deep *saikeirei* bow, tipping yourself over from the waist at a 45-degree angle (it's best not performed after sipping too much saké, although that's precisely when you might need it most).

Similarly, if you really make a mess of things in **China**, you could try and rescue the situation by kowtowing to the offended party (kneeling down, with your forehead on the floor).

associated with wishing for good luck, or to get out of a promise – is considered an obscene gesture in **Vietnam**, where the symbol represents female genitalia. ☀ In **Bulgaria**, shaking your head from side to side means yes, while nodding up and down means no. Or does it? Yes, no – we think so. It's confusing. ☀ The chin flick is an effective – albeit rude – way to tell someone to get lost, or let them know you're bored, in **Italy**, **France**, **Belgium** and **Tunisia**. ☀ You're unlikely to do this one accidentally, but in **India** and **Pakistan**, the action of putting your thumb in your mouth and flicking it out is known as the *cutis*, and it translates to 'F*** you and your entire family...' ☀ In **Arabic** and **Caribbean** nations, using the index finger on one hand to point at the five fingers on the opposite hand is known as the 'five fathers', and it implies your mother is promiscuous.

SPACE AND TOUCH

Most people are a bit protective about their personal space and no one wants a stranger right up in it, but there are variations to what is considered normal and acceptable around the world. In **Northern Europe**, **North America** and most of **Asia**, people prefer to keep a good 20in (50cm) or so between themselves and others, whereas in **Southern Europe** (**Italy**, **Greece** and **Spain**, for example), **Latin America**, the **Middle East**, parts of **Africa** and in **India**, that distance will often be halved. Repeatedly touching people is also more common in countries where locals come in close, and in **Italy**, pushing past people is not considered rude at all (so there's no point complaining about it).

Of course, there are other ways to greet people beyond handshakes, air kisses and bows. In **New Zealand/Aotearoa** and right across **Polynesia**, the honi (or hongi) sees people press their noses together while closing their eyes, and a similar greeting is used in **Yemen** and **Kuwait**. In **Greenland**, this kind of 'nose kiss' is called a *kunik*, but you might also experience people rubbing their nose against your face or neck while inhaling deeply as a way to say hello.

✸ HELPFUL ✸
DOS AND DON'TS
WHEN TALKING TO STRANGERS

DO make an effort to speak the local language, at least learning how to say hello, goodbye, please, thank you, sorry and help!

DON'T shout. There's no need – seriously. Talking slower might help, but dialing up the volume helps no one

DO follow locals' lead when working out whether to accompany a greeting with a kiss, hug or handshake.

DON'T inflict pain on people when shaking their hand – it's not a power play.

DO look people straight in the eye during greetings and toasts, but...

DON'T stare into the other person's eyes when bowing in Asia; look at your shoes instead.

DO be mindful that hand gestures you use at home might mean something radically different in other countries, and could be perceived as offensive regardless of your intent.

DON'T offer your left hand in greeting.

CHAPTER FOUR

MEALS, SNACKS & DRINKS

DINING & DRINKING

The markets, menus, restaurants and eating and drinking habits of a destination tell you plenty about the place you're exploring, and present excellent opportunities to bond with your hosts.

WE ALL NEED TO EAT AND DRINK, and sharing culinary experiences with others is one of the best parts of traveling. Many cultures revolve centrifugally around favored foods, and sometimes the act of preparing, serving and imbibing certain substances is transformed into something that resembles a ritual or artform – take the tea ceremony in **Japan**, a procedure so saturated in symbolism it can last up to four hours; or the traditional *kava* ceremony in **Fiji**, which feels more like a rite of passage than a drinking session.

The markets, menus, restaurants and eating and drinking habits of a destination tell you plenty about the place you're exploring, and present excellent opportunities to bond with your hosts. Sharing a cup of *yerba mate* with locals in **Argentina** is a peak South American travel experience, as is dipping chunks of bread into a communal caldron filled with creamy, cheesy fondue in **Alpine Switzerland**.

But mealtimes abroad also present the faux-pas-prone traveler with ample opportunity for embarrassment. In fact, few scenarios are as likely to end up with you having egg on your face than when you're attempting to navigate unfamiliar manners and eating traditions. Wearing your food is frowned upon everywhere, but nearly everything else – from belching to licking your plate clean – is acceptable somewhere around the globe, despite being considered disgusting some place else. Here's how to avoid committing the most egregious gastronomic gaffes.

Navigating New Cuisines

Trying new food is an exciting part of traveling, so be brave and dive in. Except when you need the toilet, avoid frequenting big international chains you can visit at home, and instead try locally owned places where the country's traditional cuisine is served.

Food markets and suburbs with street vendors are vibrant places to explore, often sending you on a sensory adventure through winding alleyways permeated with delicious scents, and can be as much of a sightseeing opportunity as a mealtime destination. Fruit and vegetable markets are also fascinating, full of fresh produce you've likely never seen or sampled before. If I close my eyes, I can still taste the freshly-pressed sugarcane juice and sensational seafood I scarfed at Darajani Market in Stone Town, **Zanzibar**, or smell the great bowls of aromatic spices in the souks of **Oman** and **Morocco**.

If possible, take a food-tasting tour with a guide or, even better, sign up for a cooking course, where your host can educate you about the history and stories behind signature dishes and drinks. (And they'll likely be able to teach you the local table manners that'll save you a few blushes down the line.)

People are generally proud of their cuisine, and pleased when visitors try local specialties, but there's no point going for the hundred-year-old egg in **China**, trying a deep-fried tarantula in **Cambodia** or ordering *cuy al horno* (spit-roasted guinea pig) in **Peru** if you then recoil when it's presented to you on a plate – that can cause offense. And if you go to the Surströmming Festival – an eating event in **Sweden** also known as the 'Festival of Rotten Fish'

– then you really should know what you're getting yourself into.

MENUS AND ORDERING

Menus can be intimidating when you're somewhere new and unfamiliar. Don't be afraid to ask owners, cooks and wait staff for assistance and pointers, especially if you want to try local dishes. If staff are especially sniffy and snooty (certain destinations have a real reputation for such behavior – yes, we're talking about *you*, **France**), don't sit there and suffer it. Walk out and find somewhere nicer – it's their loss. (Just be aware that in small towns and villages there might not be many options – you don't want to have to slink back in, tail between legs, if everywhere else is full, shut, or shockingly bad.)

BEST PRACTICES

AVOIDING MENU MISHAPS

* While entrée means main course in **the USA**, in **France** (and pretty much everywhere else) it refers to a starter or appetizer.

* Ordering a set meal, or *table d'hôte* (French for 'the host's table'), where you're served a number of courses for a fixed price, can be a good, cost-effective and easy option.

* If you want to select courses *à la carte* (off the menu), ask staff for a recommendation (and be advised that this will not be the cheapest ordering strategy).

* In many countries, including **Korea**, **Italy**, **Ethiopia** and **Thailand**, communal dining and sharing meals from the same serving dish is common – buddy up with someone local and benefit from their knowledge.

* Ordering mixed plates – mezes in **Türkiye**, tapas in **Spain**, dim sum in **China** – allows you to sample many different dishes.

Make friends with fellow travelers and locals (see p. 53) and invite them to eat with you, so you can pick their brains about the best local cuisine and learn about regional manners and traditions. Failing that, indulge in some people-watching: pick a well-populated restaurant, look around and see what dishes other people are enjoying (except in **Egypt**, where it's considered rude to gawp at other people's plates), and request the same. Two caveats here: avoid pointing too blatantly (a major faux-pas in some cultures; see p. 66) and double check the price; the Fourchu lobster or bluefin tuna sashimi may look amazing, but the bill might be gut-churning if you're still getting the hang of the conversion rate.

EATING ETHICS

As exciting as it may be to try new foods, it's a good rule of thumb to avoid dishes containing parts of endangered animals, or which are harvested in dangerous, cruel or unsustainable ways, such as shark fin soup (found on menus in **China** and **Southeast Asia**) and various kinds of bushmeat (which can range from monkey meat to bats in various street food dishes). While it's legal to eat *foie gras* in **France**, sea turtle in the **Cayman Islands** and whale meat in **Iceland**, **Norway**, **Japan** and the **Faroe Islands** (not to mention seafood caught by highly destructive factory ships in the **UK** and **US**), it's worth considering the ethics behind how these foods are harvested before you tuck in.

You may encounter menus with meat sourced from animals that you find deeply upsetting, from dolphins to dogs. This can be challenging if you're a vegan, vegetarian or pescatarian—some cultures and cuisines are simply more carnivorous than others—but often people are just working with what they've got. Order according to your dietary needs as best you can, but no matter how well-meaning you may be, lecturing locals about their traditional diet is rude, and will definitely ruffle feathers (no one wants to hear a tourist get on their soapbox about the ethics of meat eating, especially in a country that's experienced food scarcity). If you have strong feelings about these issues, do your research and make informed decisions about where to travel.

TOP TIP

If the menu is especially perplexing and there's no one able or willing to help, there are plenty of apps for translating menus.

Making Reservations

Don't assume everyone everywhere eats at the same time as you do back home. In the **USA**, **Canada**, **Germany**, **France**, **Belgium** and **Britain**, most people have their evening meal between 6pm and 7pm, but in **Finland**, the **Netherlands** and **Norway** it's not uncommon to tuck in at 5pm or earlier; in **Italy**, **Greece**, **Portugal**, **Croatia**, **South Africa** and especially **Spain** and **Argentina**, no one starts scoffing dinner until 9pm or later. The mere thought of this might give you indigestion, but when in **Rome**... (or **Madrid**, **Lisbon**, **Buenos Aires**) it's worth taking into account unless you want to be eating in empty restaurants. But in **Mediterranean** countries, make sure you don't have lunch too early (or line up some afternoon snacks), otherwise you're going to be hangry as hell by 9pm.

When dining at people's homes, turning up at the appropriate time can be trickier than you might think. In **Austria**, **Germany**, **Britain**, **South Africa**, **Japan**, **Switzerland**, **China** and **Iran** you should try and arrive exactly at the agreed time, while in the **Philippines**, **Portugal**, **Russia** and **Ireland** you can be a little bit late (15 minutes or so), but in **Argentina**, **Brazil** and **Mexico** it's positively rude to arrive on time – turn up at least 30 minutes after you said you would.

Minding Your Manners

There's more to good manners than keeping your elbows off the table (if there is one) and not talking with your mouth full (which is actually fine in some places). In a great many countries across **Asia** and the **Middle East**, including **India**, **Kenya**, **Malaysia** and **Morocco**, you should avoid picking up food or – worse – handing food to someone else with your left hand (which is associated with toilet duties and considered less clean).

Sometimes what's seen as positive in one place is regarded as rude somewhere else. In **India** and **Japan**, if you fail to completely clean your plate it's frowned upon, but across **China** and **Russia**, and in **Thailand**, the **Philippines** and **Egypt**, if you gobble everything up it implies you weren't given enough food (which is offensive), so you should leave a little bit. Noisily slurping your noodles is frowned upon in countries like **South Korea** and **Singapore**, but absolutely encouraged in **Japan**, **China** and **Cambodia** (where it should be accompanied by lip-smacking). And that's before we get on to loudly burping after a meal (deemed a sign of appreciation in **China**) and farting, the equivalent in some Inuit cultures in **Canada**.

But there are myriad rules according to the country you're in, including the following:

TOP TIP

Only the coolest people have the chops to travel alone, and when you're flying solo you shouldn't miss the best eating options a destination has to offer. Food markets are ideal places for solo travelers to score great food on the move. If you actively don't want to be surrounded by couples and groups, hit restaurants early or make lunch your main meal.

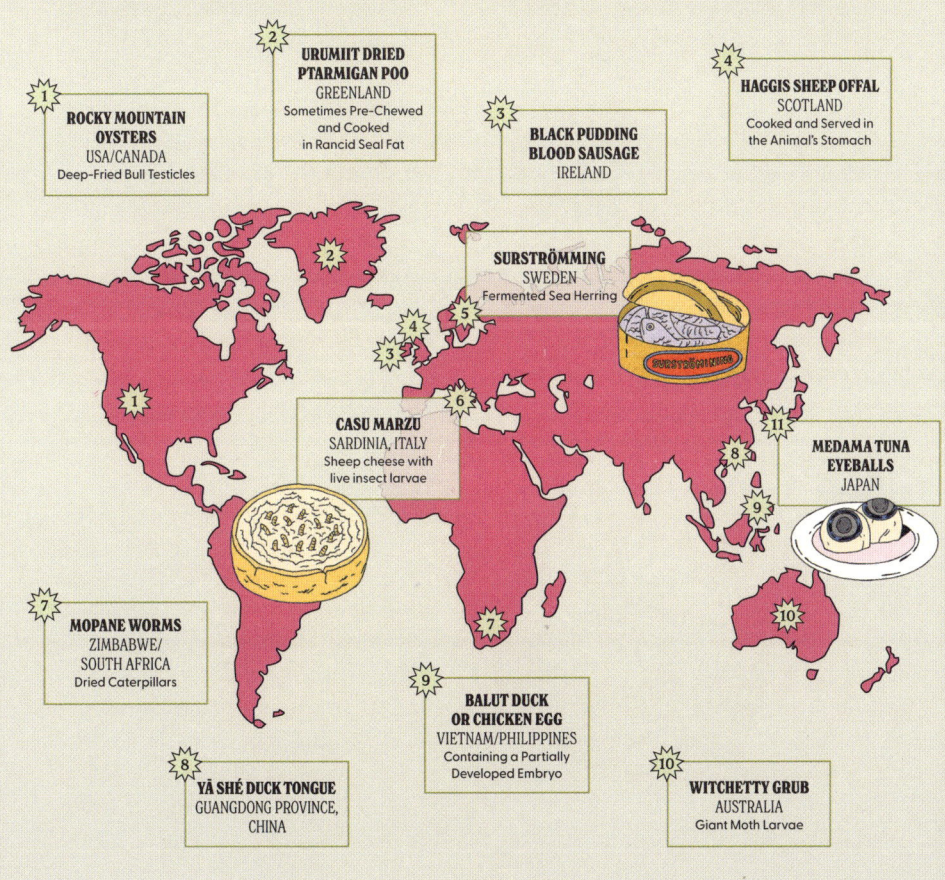

✺ In **Italy**, never cut your pasta (but also don't make a slurping noise while sucking it into your mouth); and if cheese isn't offered with the dish, don't ask for it sprinkled on top. ✺ When eating whole fish in **southern China** and **Hong Kong**, flipping it over is considered bad luck (because it symbolizes a boat capsizing). ✺ In **Thailand**, forks are only used to push food towards your spoon – putting a fork in your mouth is akin to eating straight off a knife in the **UK** and **USA**. ✺ When invited to barbecues in **Australia**, it's customary to 'bring a plate'; don't arrive with a personal piece of crockery, just bring some food (that the host will then cook). ✺ Don't use cutlery to eat tacos in **Mexico**, pizzas in **Italy**, or burgers in the **USA**. ✺ Never leave the table while others are still eating in **Nepal**. ✺ Don't point chopsticks at people in **Japan** (an act of aggression), and avoid passing food from one pair of chopsticks to another – an action similar to a funeral tradition. ✺ In **China**, never leave chopsticks standing upright in a bowl of rice – this is reminiscent of a ritual performed when people make offerings to the dead. ✺ Bread is not an appetizer in **France**, it's intended to accompany your food. ✺ Licking your fingers is considered very rude in **Ethiopia** and **Chile**. ✺ Wait staff in **Egypt** or **Portugal** will be unimpressed (and chefs incandescent) if you ask for salt and pepper. ✺ If an older person offers you a drink or a bowl or plate of food in **Korea**, receive it with both hands to show respect. ✺ In **France** and **Chile**, you should always keep your hands above the table (dropping them is seen as bad manners).

HOW TO DRESS FOR DINNER

Dress codes for restaurants, bars and bistros vary enormously within countries and cities, let alone across the globe. If strict guidelines are in place, they should be made clear, but generally speaking, the posher the place the more effort you need to make. Looking presentable is a sign of

respect for your hosts, and even when eating in budget venues. If you're in any doubt, err on the side of caution and dress smartly but comfortably.

That said, many traditional restaurants in **Japan** prefer diners to remove their shoes, and will provide slippers to be worn inside the premises (BYO slippers if you prefer, or if you have large feet). Of course there are many shorts-and-barefoot-friendly beach-based restaurants in ocean-facing destinations from **Australia**, **Fiji** and the **Cook Islands** to the **Caribbean** and **Greece**, but don't assume that all establishments in such ostensibly laid-back places will be cool with you rocking up in your bikini or board shorts.

WHEN TO START EATING

In **Argentina**, **Kenya**, **Italy**, **Greece** and **Singapore**, you should not begin eating until your host starts, while elsewhere (including in **Korea**, **Vietnam**, **Cambodia**, **Ethiopia** and **India**), it's the eldest person in the group or room who should take the first bite. Many cultures use a verbal cue that chomping can commence: 'Guten Appetit' (**Germany**); 'Bon appetit' (**France**); 'Itadakimasu' (**Japan**); 'Buon appetite' (**Italy**); 'Bom apetite' (**Portugal**); 'Tuck in!' (**Britain**); 'Buen Provecho!' (**Mexico**); 'Head itsu' (**Estonia**).

KEEPING YOUR COOL

THAT'S NOT WHAT I ORDERED...

When you're in a new place, attempting to decipher a menu you're not familiar with, the chances of a communication breakdown are high. Try enlisting the help of staff from the beginning, and be friendly and polite – because that's always the best way to behave, and they will be much more inclined to assist if things go awry. If your meal comes and it's nothing like you expected, you can: a) embrace serendipity and scoff it anyway (you might discover your new favorite dish); b) attempt to swap plates with a friend or fellow traveler (preferably with their consent), or c) try sending it back, courteously explaining your reasons for doing so (do this immediately – good luck returning a half-chewed meal...). As a rule, the more upmarket the venue, the pickier you can be.

TRAVEL ETIQUETTE TIPS

In Italy, never cut yo
don't make a slurpi
sucking it into your
isn't offered with th
for it sprinkled on t

r pasta (but also
g noise while
outh); and if cheese
 dish, don't ask
p.

Drinking

TRAVEL ETIQUETTE TIPS

Whether you're quaffing coffee, sipping tea, sniffing wine, shooting spirits or clinking beers, the customs and rituals that whirl around countries' drinking cultures are as complex as they are fascinating. Across large parts of the globe alcoholic drinks are not sold or served (and it's important not to flaunt local laws about booze). But everywhere has an elixir of choice: a drink, alcoholic or otherwise, which helps define the destination. Here are a few golden rules to keep in mind as you guzzle your way around the globe:

✺ Never order a cappuccino after mid-morning in **Italy**, where milky coffee is a breakfast drink. From 11am onwards, it's hardcore espressos only. ✺ In **France**, don't refill your wine glass without first offering a splash to everyone else around the table.

✺ Pouring wine with your left hand is considered rude in **Argentina** and **Bolivia**. ✺ In **South Korea**, your glass should be empty before being refilled; and it's not customary for women to pour drinks for other women. ✺ When drinking with other people in **Britain** or **Ireland**, be sure to get your round in (buying a drink for everyone with you who wants one). ✺ In many countries, including **Japan** and **Egypt**, it's impolite

TOP TIP

Tempting as it is, snagging a cool glass as a souvenir of your travels is still stealing. In **Britain**, lost glasses are estimated to cost the hospitality industry £186 million a year, and we've heard of one joint in **Belgium** (where many of the beer glasses are *very* cool) that insists punters leave a shoe behind the bar as a 'deposit' for glasses – a clever way of addressing the problem. If you really want a particular glass, ask bar staff if you can buy one.

CHEERS!

SHOULD I BRING THAT BOTTLE OF WINE TO DINNER?

Nothing is more nerve-racking than choosing a bottle of wine for a dinner party in France, where everyone is a virtuoso in vino appreciation. For starters, make sure to ask the host for guidance—you don't want to turn up with a Cabernet if they're planning on serving mussels (you'll also score extra points for selecting a wine from the host's home region.) Secondly, don't buy something you've never had or don't know about—you're better off asking the shop owner for a recommendation than flying blind. Lastly, don't skimp on the price (no need to bankrupt yourself with a bottle of 1998 Domaine Leroy Romanee-Saint-Vivant Grand Cru, but don't expect to win any friends with a €5 screw-top).

to pour your own drinks (unless you're dining alone). ✹ It's rude to turn down a drink in **Russia**, where the offer is a sign of friendship. If that drink is a shot of vodka, be sure to down it in one.
✹ In **Iran**, the *taarof* tradition means you should initially turn down offers of tea (and other sweets and treats) even if you want them – fear not, your host will continue to insist until you accept.
✹ In **Georgia**, you don't sip wine steadily – it's traditional to drink it during toasts only. ✹ In **Argentina**, when offered a slurp of *mate* (sucked through a straw stuck in a shared cup), turning it down can cause offense – it's a sign of friendship. ✹ Never order a 'black and tan' (a mix of stout and paler ale) in **Ireland**, where the name is historically associated with a paramilitary force that committed some of the worst atrocities

in the country's War of Independence. (If you must drink this monstrosity, best to call it a 'half-and-half'.) ❁ In **Kazakhstan**, take it as a compliment if your host only half fills your *piala* (bowl) with tea – this indicates they want you to stay for several cups and enjoy a longer conversation.

ALE FAILS

While **France** is famously wine obsessed, appreciation of beer is tantamount to a religion across the rest of **northern Europe**, especially in **Belgium**, **Czechia**, **Germany**, **Britain** and **Ireland**. There are hundreds of styles, thousands of breweries and countless varieties. Simply requesting 'a beer' doesn't help bar staff, and makes you look like a complete beginner. It's fine to ask the bartender to suggest something local, just choose a moment when they're not trying to contend with a thirsty crowd. Many bartenders will offer you a small taster of the local brew, to see if you like it before ordering a large glass.

MAKING TOASTS

Proposing a toast is an integral part of communal and celebratory drinking sessions the world over, but there are often unwritten rules around who calls them and when, according to where you are (in a house or a bar) and who you are (host or visitor), so don't just climb on a table and start raising your drink and voice. In **Russia**, no eating or drinking starts until a toast (or two) has happened, and visitors go first. In **Japan**, however, only the host raises a toast (and guests shouldn't reciprocate). In **Denmark** and **Finland**, the host makes the initial toast, and no drinking should take place until this has happened. In **Germany**, there are different toasts according to what you're drinking –'*Zum wohl*' for wine and '*Prost*' for beer – but whatever you're drinking, it's very important to look the other person in the eye, or risk several years of bad luck (or bad sex, as some people now say).

In **Hungary**, never clink beer glasses during a toast; this tradition ceased after the failed 1848–49 Hungarian Revolution, when officers of the Austrian Habsburg Empire were seen celebrating the defeat and subsequent execution of Hungarian patriots.

TOP TIP

There are as many ways to say cheers as there are languages on Earth, but one golden rule exists all around the planet: when your glasses make contact and you utter the toast, make sure you are looking your drinking buddy straight in the eye.

Tipping

Tips will absolutely be expected in diners, cafes, bars and restaurants across the **Americas** (think 15–20% for meals, and a dollar or two for drinks) – if you forget to fork out, don't even think about returning.

Even in many countries where tipping is not customary – such as **Britain**, **Ireland**, **Australia** and **New Zealand/Aotearoa** – leaving a little something for wait staff in restaurants is common practice, and certainly won't upset or embarrass anyone. In continental **Europe** the situation is similar (wait staff in **Scandinavian** countries might be surprised, mainly because not many visitors have much money left after paying the bill), but in all of these places, minimum wages are paid, so staff are not reliant on gratuities – also, a service charge may get automatically added to your bill, so check first. The situation is very different in parts of **Asia**, though. While tipping people in **India**, **Sri Lanka**, **Thailand** and across **Southeast Asia** is fine (many are poorly paid), trying to give restaurant or bar staff money in **Japan** and **Korea** can bewilder and embarrass them, so don't do it.

TOP TIP

In **France**, offer to pay the whole bill or accept the other person's offer – it's considered unseemly to split the cost of a meal. In **Thailand**, the wealthiest person at the table picks up the bill, while in **Austria**, whoever extended the invite pays. In **the Netherlands**, you really do go Dutch and split the bill.

✺ HELPFUL ✺ DOS AND DON'TS

WHEN DINING & DRINKING

DO follow locals' lead when wondering when to start eating.

DON'T make a disgusted face after trying a local delicacy.

DO avoid slurping, burping and farting at the table – unless you know for an absolute fact that it's seen as a sign of appreciation.

DON'T leave your glass empty if you don't want more to drink. In many places it will be refilled immediately.

DO always compliment your host on the meal.

DON'T ask for ketchup in European restaurants (*Sacre bleu* – the chef spent hours creating that sauce, you philistine!).

DO avoid taking the last morsel of food from a shared plate (unless your host absolutely insists).

DON'T rush. In lots of countries eating is about savoring the experience and enjoying both the meal and the company, not seeking fast food.

CHAPTER FIVE

SIGHTS, LINES & SELFIES

VISITING LOCAL SITES

We are primarily drawn to far-flung destinations to explore spectacular sights, ranging from culture-defining castles, cathedrals, temples, shrines, museums and monuments through to epic national parks, fantastic flora and fauna, and sensational natural wonders.

THESE UNIQUE PLACES AND ENCOUNTERS are made all the more alluring by the aura that surrounds them – so the very last thing a conscientious traveler wants to do is ruin the experience for fellow explorers or, worse still, inadvertently shatter the sacred solemnity of a site and upset the local custodians.

The way you conduct yourself while traveling is important – like it or not, you're an ambassador for your own country and culture. And sometimes it isn't as simple as not sauntering around sacred sites butt naked, or avoiding dropping litter. For example, wandering and standing with your hands in your pockets symbolizes arrogance in **Japan** and **Korea**, and is deemed deeply disrespectful if you're doing it in front of a monument, shrine or place of cultural significance. In **Thailand** (and many other parts of **Asia**), where feet are considered the lowliest part of the body, pointing your toes towards sacred objects in temples is enormously offensive. In **Greece**, wearing high heels is prohibited when touring ancient monuments such as the Parthenon and the Acropolis in **Athens**.

Technically it's also illegal to frown in **Milan, Italy**, to swear in **New South Wales, Australia** or fart in a public place after 6pm in **Florida, USA** – but you'll probably get away with breaking some of those rules if you're discreet. Regardless, what follows is a bit of guidance on how not to make an absolute spectacle of yourself while sightseeing.

Navigating Lines and Queues

TRAVEL ETIQUETTE TIPS

Famously, forming an orderly queue is a national pastime in **Britain** and anyone foolish enough to push in can expect a very hard stare. Questions about the etiquette of queuing are included in the Citizen Test for migrants attempting to move to the UK, and the legendary queue for Wimbledon tennis tickets has its own webpage (there's actually a Queue Village with refreshments on sale and big screens for watching tennis while you wait).

But the British are not alone in respecting the need to politely stand in line. Taking one's proper turn is firmly ingrained in the culture of **Japan** (where no one would dream of cutting the queue), and it's common practice in the **USA** too (although in true capitalist form, you can pay extra to skip the worst of the queues in places like

Disneyland). In **Thailand**, local people leave their shoes or flipflops in the queue, and go off and do more interesting stuff until the line starts moving.

While traveling, however, you will certainly encounter cultures where the concept of queuing is utterly alien. In **China**, **Italy**, **Israel** and **India**, for example, people never line up in an orderly fashion. Fortune favors the brave in such places, so you have to learn to quicken your wits, sharpen your elbows and set your focus firmly on whatever the goal or prize is.

TOP TIP

The Canadian School of Protocol and Etiquette in Ontario, Canada offers 'queue training', teaching newcomers to North America the proper way to keep their place and how close to stand to the person in front of them.

YES, IT'S A THING

THE DOS AND DON'TS OF STROKING STATUES

In some cities around the world, tourist traditions such as rubbing statues are causing repair costs and consternation. Authorities in **Dublin**, **Ireland** recently placed stewards on the street to stop people from touching the bronze breasts of the city's beloved *Molly Malone* statue (a tribute to women who sold shellfish on the streets of the Irish capital); such behavior – which allegedly brings luck – was inflicting several thousand Euro of damage to the artwork every month.

But poor Molly isn't the only stone character to endure such indignities. Similar traditions include rubbing the crotch of Victor Noir's recumbent effigy in the Père Lachaise Cemetery in **Paris** to seek fertility; touching the breast of the Juliet statue in **Verona**, **Italy**, to bring luck in love (clearly by people unfamiliar with the plot of *Romeo and Juliet*); and, to bring good luck, touching the testicles of the *Charging Bull* in **New York**.

TRAVEL ETIQUETTE TIPS

Never light fires out
spots, not least beca
spark can destroy a
a whole generation.
to make like a bear i
a pit, and do it well
source that people

ide of designated
use a careless
 entire area for
nd if you have
 the woods, dig
way from a water
ight be using.

VISITING LOCAL SITES

Exhibiting Your Best Behavior

TRAVEL ETIQUETTE TIPS

Art galleries and museums are often a window into the soul of a culture – these buildings are treasure troves of learning, where a country's best and worst historical events are retold, and the fruits of the people's creativity and innovation are on display (or, in the case of the British Museum in **London**, where loot from centuries of colonial acquisition can be seen). Places like the Uffizi in **Florence**, the Louvre in **Paris**, MoMA in **New York**, MALBA in **Buenos Aires**, and the Museum of Qin Terracotta Warriors in **Xi'an** top the list of attractions that draw visitors to a destination in the first place. But once you get inside, there are ways to behave beyond not running, squealing or touching stuff with gelato-gooey hands.

Do you have strong opinions about something on display? Awesome – that's the whole point, but perhaps discuss it quietly with whoever you're with rather than sharing your erudite opinions with the entire hall. Not everyone appreciates the finer qualities of Cubism, but loudly announcing that a Picasso painting is similar to 'the type of trash my four-year-old brings home from elementary school' really won't win you fans or enhance other people's enjoyment of the Museo Reina Sofía in **Madrid**.

If you're taking pictures, remember to turn the flash off – lots of galleries operate a no-photography policy, too, so note all the signage. Also, standing

TOP TIP
Thinking about sneaking a photo in a camera-free exhibition? Many museum gift shops sell souvenirs featuring professional photographs of the collection's highlights. Wouldn't you rather have a gorgeous postcard than a blurry stealth shot?

really close to, and directly in front of, objects and artwork means other people can see more of your backside than they can the display (and no matter how hot you think your derrière is, I'm willing to bet it's no oil painting compared to that Rembrandt or Van Gogh).

Checking out a smaller museum or gallery is an excellent way to kill some time while waiting to catch a train or plane to your next destination, but wobbling around a space full of fragile and priceless artifacts with a pack on your back, like a lost and dizzy tortoise, is a recipe for disaster (and annoying for other visitors). Most places will have lockers you can stick your luggage in before exploring the exhibits, but make sure to check the museum's website first and plan accordingly.

CONTINUED

THE DOS AND DON'TS OF STROKING STATUES

In the grand scheme of things, there are worse cultural crimes tourists could be committing, but treating religious effigies with such presumptuous familiarity should certainly be avoided: in 2015, three men were given jail sentences in **Myanmar (Burma)** for posting a Facebook image of a Buddha wearing headphones.

Visiting Religious Sites

If you only care to wear sleeves once or twice during your entire hedonistic odyssey around the world, make it those times you choose to visit a cathedral, temple, mosque or shrine. Nothing upsets people more than the sight of disrespectful tourists flaunting their bare skin around sacred sites, and in some places, people will deny you entry unless you cover up. What counts as acceptable attire varies from place to place, but both men and women can safely assume that shoulders and knees should be covered, whether you're visiting Buddhist sites in **Cambodia**, Hindu temples in **India**, a mosque in **Oman**, a Catholic cathedral in **Spain** (especially on holy days) or a beach-based Sunday church service in **Fiji**. Often women will also need to cover their hair, while men might be expected to remove headwear like baseball caps. Be mindful of the imagery displayed on what you wear, too – a Megadeth hoodie emblazoned with skulls might cover you up, but it won't win you any admiring looks from locals paying respects to lost loved ones.

Many religious sites, such as the beautiful Blue Mosque in **İstanbul**, **Türkiye**, actively welcome male and female visitors, and will provide garments such as headscarves if you haven't come prepared, but don't assume you can just wander up to any place of worship while you are traveling and pop your head in – very often there are strict rules about entering such places. If in doubt, always inquire at your accommodation or ask a local whether it's possible to visit a temple or shrine on a certain day or time.

A LINE CHART

IS THAT LINE WORTH THE WAIT?

5 MINUTES
A basic cup of coffee

15 MINUTES
An amusement park ride

30 MINUTES
New video game release

1 HOUR
Meet n' greet with your favorite celebrity

1 DAY
Free tickets to a sold-out show

1 WEEK
Heaven's Gates

Where Not to Wear Your Swimsuit

While most people are aware of sensitivities around wearing revealing clothing in certain regions, there are some surprising places where you can get into more trouble than you might expect for sauntering around in skimpy attire.

When it was first invented in the mid 20th century, the bikini (named, bizarrely, after an atoll where nuclear testing was taking place) caused an explosion of moral outrage, and was quickly banned on beaches, around swimming pools and in public places ranging from **Italy**, **Spain** and **Portugal** to **Australia**. While navel-baring bathing suits have since become de rigeur on beaches (and at carnivals) from **Copacabana** in **Brazil** to **Bondi** in **Australia**, some destinations have more recently revived rules that strongly discourage tourists from taking to the town in their two-pieces.

It's against the law to wear bikinis, swimming trunks or to go bare-chested away from the beachfront area in **Barcelona, Spain**. In **Croatia**, there is a 'bikini ban' in the historic Old City of **Dubrovnik**, with signs at the three main entrances into the UNESCO World Heritage site warning that wearing swimwear in the streets will result in a hefty fine; similar rules are in place on the island of **Hvar**, further along the Dalmatian coast. In southern **Italy**, the spectacular town of **Sorrento** (which overlooks the Bay of Naples), also inflicts fines on anyone walking the streets in revealing swimwear or topless. In the **Maldives** (a Muslim country), revealing swimwear is restricted to certain beaches, which are cordoned off. In the **USA**, where each beach seems to have its own laws about toplessness and naturism (especially along the ocean-stroked coasts of **California**, **Florida**, and **New York**), local authorities have pondered long and hard over the conundrum of deciding what tips over into actual nudity, resulting in some *extremely specific* rules about the percentage of flesh that can be on display. (If you're visiting, do some research, and take advice from locals.)

There are claims that it's illegal to wear a bikini while singing in the state of **Florida**, but while there haven't been *that* many arrests for such acts, maybe avoid crooning in your skimpies, just in case. On the other hand, in many municipal swimming pools in **France**, baggy shorts are banned for men – it's compulsory to wear tight-fitting swimming trunks. Depending on how varied your travels are, it's probably best to bring a couple options.

WHEN CLOTHES GET LOST IN TRANSLATION

While nakedness can be naughty (and illegal), some clothing can be unexpectedly controversial. Civilians are banned from wearing camouflage-patterned garments in various places – including many Caribbean countries (**Jamaica**, **Barbados**, **Trinidad & Tobago**), in **Africa** (**Nigeria**, **Zambia** and **Zimbabwe**)

and the Middle East (**Oman** and **Saudi Arabia**) because it looks too similar to official uniforms. Be cautious about wearing clothes that feature symbols which might have a strongly negative cultural connotation or historical relevance in the country or region you are traveling in, such as a hammer and sickle in **Poland**, **Hungary** (and most of **Eastern Europe** and the former Soviet Bloc). Flags, sports gear, and even certain colors can be inflammatory too, especially if you happen to be in town when a local match is being played between two bitter rivals, such as the Celtic and Rangers in **Scotland** (a long-standing feud with a vicious sectarian backdrop), Fenerbahçe vs Galatasaray in **Türkiye**, Boca Juniors vs River Plate in **Argentina**, or Ajax vs Feyenoord in the **Netherlands**.

Exercising Selfie Control

TRAVEL ETIQUETTE TIPS

In popular destinations, dodging people taking selfies has transformed walking along some streets into a slalom exercise, and lots of locals are heartily sick of the sight of selfie sticks (sometimes known as 'Narcissus' wand'). In this Instagram era, the practice is so problematic it has prompted local authorities to bring in new laws: in **Las Vegas** tourists face a fine of up to US$1000 for loitering on bridges taking photos of themselves (which is a bit rich, in a city where there is an actual Museum of Selfies). In **Italy**, the congestion conundrum is so acute that **Portofino** on the Italian Riviera has brought in no-waiting zones (complete with fines) to avoid happy snappers blocking the way; and in **Rome**, **Florence** and **Venice**, temporary stop lights for pedestrians have been installed in busy areas.

Garoupe Beach in **southern France** has completely banned selfies, in an admirable (and optimistic) bid to encourage visitors to live in the moment, while in the **USA**, authorities in **California** have outlawed selfie-taking in the Lake Tahoe region for a very different reason: bears are common in this area of the Sierra Nevada Mountains, and many visitors were risking their lives to get a photo of themselves with the animals in the background (which sounds a lot like Darwinism in action).

Posing for a selfie in front of a deity at a sacred site ups the ante considerably and can also land you in serious trouble. In **Sri Lanka**, it's illegal to take selfies with your back turned to Buddha statues, and anyone posting pictures of themselves assuming a yoga pose in front of Buddhist effigies anywhere risks a complete loss of respect and potential ostracism.

TOP TIP

Don't pay to get photos taken with dangerous animals (such as tigers in **India** – they're almost certainly drugged up and held in terrible living conditions), or pay money to people who make animals do tricks; it's highly likely that 'dancing' bears or 'painting' elephants are being subjected to unethical training methods and poor living conditions.

A QUESTION

CAN I PET THE CUTE KOALA?

No. Really, please don't. Wildlife is wild (clue is in the name) and should not be handled – so turn off your live stream and put that baby wombat down. Lots of animals, especially in **Australia** (but also across **Africa**, **Asia** and **the Americas**), have their own way of telling you they don't want to be touched by opportunistic tourists with no respect for personal space, and if you get scratched, stung, skewered, gouged, gored or generally chewed because you tried to pick up, or pet an animal that just wanted to be left alone – that's on you. But even if you escape such encounters without being harmed, the creature you molested might not be so lucky – lots of young animals are abandoned by parents after being handled by humans, and others are left damaged or distressed. Don't do it.

Outdoor Explorations

Exploring city sights is one thing, but to really experience a country, meet its true inhabitants and encounter the wildlife, you absolutely need to go beyond the urban jungle and into the countryside.

READING AND HEEDING SIGNS

How rules, rights and freedoms are organized in wilderness areas obviously varies massively. In **Scotland** and **Scandinavia**, extremely liberal laws about the right to roam – known in the latter as *Allemansrätten* (every man's right) – mean you can walk, run, forage for food, pitch a tent, hike and bike almost anywhere you like, but no such liberty exists in **Britain**, **Ireland** and across much of the rest of **Europe** (or, indeed the rest of the world). As such, you will need to look out for signage at trailheads and while trekking (or cycling, kayaking, canoeing – whatever you're up to) to ensure you don't put yourself at risk of encountering angry landowners, aggressive and potentially deadly animals and other hazards. There are too many varieties of these to list here, but if you see a sign featuring a skull and crossbones, a gun, a symbol of an activity with a line through it, or an image of an angry bear/crocodile/snake/shark/tiger/hippo or other large and lethal-looking beast, it's probably best to turn around, look at the map for an alternative route, or at least proceed with extreme caution.

TOP TIP

In the **USA**, the unofficial holiday of National Hike Naked Day is celebrated on the summer solstice (around June 21), with nude walkers taking to popular trails including sections of the iconically popular Pacific Crest Trail (PCT) and Appalachian Trail (AT).

DON'T HIKE NAKED IN SWITZERLAND (AT LEAST IN APPENZELL)

As a rule, people are relatively relaxed about nakedness in **Switzerland**; there are several nudist beaches around on the landlocked county's popular swimming lakes, and sunbathers will regularly go topless in public parks. But a furor erupted in one alpine area, **Appenzell**, when a hiker wandered along a trail, past a Christian elderly care home, wearing just his boots and a backpack. Police fined the risqué rambler and the canton passed a local law banning bare ass hiking forevermore. Technically, however, bumbling along the trails in your birthday suit is not illegal elsewhere in Switzerland. And in **Germany** – where *Freikörperkultur* (free body culture) is strong, and there are no laws against getting your kit off anywhere – there are two official naked hiking trails: one in the Harz Mountains and one in Lower Saxony.

Fans of 'free hiking' (as trekking sans clothes is known) will be delighted to hear that the practice isn't precluded by any federal laws, but should be aware that local legislation takes precedence, and in some places you can definitely get fined for public indecency if you're caught catering around in the altogether. The best advice is to research

the area carefully, and stick to the quieter trails where you're less likely to meet families, church groups and other people who might not relish the prospect of following a naked hiker up a steep, craggy climb. Oh, and be sure to apply sunscreen everywhere...

LEAVE NO TRACE

The best travelers leave a destination as good as they find it, if not better, and when it comes to outdoor exploration this is especially important. If you're hiking, biking, canoeing or camping in the wilds – be it a **Bavarian Forest**, the **Australian Outback**, **Scottish**

107

Highlands, **Chilean Lake District**, **Japanese Alps**, **South African Transvaal** or the **Canadian backcountry** – it's essential to pack out everything you pack in. Never light fires outside of designated spots, not least because a careless spark can destroy an entire area for a whole generation. And if you have to make like a bear in the woods, dig a pit, and do it well away from a water source that people might be using. In some places, leave no trace means packing literally everything, including your poo, using a WAG bag. There are good reasons for this – mainly to protect fragile local flora and fauna – so if you choose to explore such remote regions, make sure you follow the stool rules.

TAKE ONLY PHOTOS

Hands-on exploration is still possible at magnificent, mysterious human-made sites around the world, from Angkor Wat in **Cambodia** to Sacsayhuamán in **Peru**, as well as natural wonders like the Giant's Causeway in **Northern Ireland** and Reed Flute Cave in **Guangxi**, **China**, but that could easily end if visitors hack parts of them off as souvenirs (and, clearly this is terrible behavior on every level). So don't do it.

Less obvious, perhaps, is the fact that you should not pocket pebbles or steal sea shells from the sea shore in places where the high tide of tourism is threatening to denude the destinations of the very thing that makes them magical places to visit. People found pinching pebbles from Lalaria Beach on Skiathos – an idyllic island in **Greece** that became a hotspot after it was featured in the *Mamma Mia* movies – are fined €900 (and there are honesty boxes for remorseful rock robbers to leave their purloined pebbles in). Councils in **England** have also threatened to fine people for taking pebbles, and it's illegal to remove shells from plenty of other places, including **Thailand** and national parks in the **USA**. Taking or traveling with conch shells and bits of coral is a big no-no.

CAN I CLIMB THIS SACRED ROCK?

In October 2019, people climbed Uluru (formerly known as Ayers Rock) in **Central Australia** for the last time (legally). The Anangu, Traditional Owners of the area for some 40,000 years, had previously spent decades asking visitors to stay off the rock, which is sacred to Indigenous people and off-limits according to Tjukurpa

(Anangu law), but many international and domestic tourists continued to climb, creating a scar on one side of the magnificent monolith, and often using the top as an open-air toilet. To make matters worse, many were not fit enough for the physically demanding ascent and there were several fatalities, which deeply upset the Anangu who, as custodians of the site, felt responsible for the wellbeing of visitors.

With the closure of the climb, the issue was resolved, but there are many more places around the world where the rights and wishes of Indigenous people are not being respected by tourists – and as a responsible traveler,

ANOTHER QUESTION

HOW ABOUT FEEDING THE BIRDS AND BABOONS?

Also a bad idea. In lots of popular destinations, pigeons can reach plague proportions when encouraged by people feeding them. In **Venice** it's illegal to feed pigeons, and you can be fined for doing the same thing in Trafalgar Square, **London**. As a general rule, avoid feeding any animals, especially in urban environments, because you're likely to either encourage dependency (bad for the creatures) or make them greedy and aggressive (awful for locals). In New Delhi, **India**, rhesus monkeys have become such a menace around the parliament and tourist hotspots that the government has taken to employing men to dress up as langurs – a larger species – to scare the rhesus away (which actually sounds like a dream job).

it's important to consider these before visiting. In **Australia,** such places include Wollumbin (Mt Warning) in **New South Wales,** a well-known bushwalking spot which is a sacred place of lore to the local Bundjalung people; St Mary Peak in **South Australia,** part of the popular Ikara (Wilpena Pound) Circuit hiking route, but also a site that's central to the Adnyamathanha creation story; and the Blue Hole in the Daintree rainforest north of Cairns in **Queensland,** which is a popular swimming spot but has been a significant women's place for the Kuku Yalanji people for millennia.

In **Wyoming** in the **USA,** most rock climbers honor an agreement with the Native American Lakota people and avoid scaling the Devils Tower (known as Bear Lodge to the Lakota) in June, to allow local tribes to hold ceremonies at the site. But the number of people breaking the 20-year-old voluntary ban is growing, and this is part of a concerning trend, with local cultures being sidelined, Indigenous names for features being discarded and protected areas – like Utah's Bears Ears National Monument – being significantly shrunk.

Whenever you're visiting a destination with an Indigenous population that has strong ties to the land – be it **Australia,** the **USA, Canada, Mexico, New Zealand/Aotearoa, Bolivia, Brazil, Peru, Papua New Guinea** or **Greenland** – one excellent way to make sure you are not treading on the toes of the Indigenous people, or trespassing on sacred land, is to engage a local guide directly connected to the native culture.

TOP TIP

The reason people are no longer allowed to get up close to the 5000-year old standing stones of Stonehenge, in the southwest of **England,** is that tourists kept climbing on them and chipping bits off to take home.

HELPFUL DOS AND DON'TS
WHEN VISITING LOCAL SITES

DO dress and act respectfully, especially around places of worship and sites of solemnity.

DON'T get naked or go topless or bare-chested unless you're very aware of local laws and cultural sensitivities.

DO follow locals' lead when it comes to queuing.

DON'T shout and run about in museums and galleries

DO be mindful about where you're pointing your feet when visiting shrines and sacred sites in Asia.

DON'T pick up or pet wild animals, or feed the birds and monkeys

DO use Leave No Trace principles when you're exploring wild areas.

DON'T ride exotic animals such as elephants or ostriches (and research horse-riding outfits before booking to ensure mounts are treated well). Never pay to see animals perform.

DO try and engage a local guide to ensure you don't unwittingly engage in activities that disrespect Indigenous land or people.

DON'T assume you can take things like pebbles or shells as free souvenirs.

CHAPTER SIX

KNICKKNACKS, GOODS & SOUVENIRS

SHOPPING

Taking memories home from your travels is one thing, 🧳 but most of us like to return with a few tangible 🏺 treasures too. ✳

THESE PURCHASES can take myriad forms, from stereotypical touristy trinkets through to unique artworks that transport you back to a much-loved destination every time you see them, or unusual objets d'art or items of folk art that you simply couldn't walk past in a market – perhaps a carved mask made by *mascareros* in **Mexico**, or an iconic tool, piece of jewelry or item of clothing with deep connections to a particular place, like an Aran jumper from the eponymous islands on the west coast of **Ireland**.

It's an undeniable fact that where and how you spend your dollar can make a massive difference, so it's important to think for a moment before splashing your cash. Has the item you're eyeing up really been made by a local artisan, or churned out by children working in terrible conditions in a completely different country thousands of miles away?

And that's before we've even mentioned the ethics of wealthy Westerners attempting to squeeze every last cent from each bartering battle, the complexity of shopping etiquette, the pros and cons of carrying cash, and the potential pitfalls of purchasing a life-sized carved wooden giraffe when your itinerary involves traveling onwards through another six southern **African** countries by bus and train.

What follows is an attempt to steer you towards some sensible decision-making techniques, and away from the worst retail riptides to get caught in.

Understanding Shop Etiquette

TRAVEL ETIQUETTE TIPS

It's tempting for travelers to take a totally different approach to shopping when they're overseas than they would at home, but the fact is, while there are cultural idiosyncrasies that make the experience different and interesting, the basic principles remain the same: you need or desire something, and a vendor or shop worker wants to sell it to you. Don't assume that just because you're in a country with lower socioeconomic living standards than your own, you can barter over the price of every purchase

TOP TIP
While cash might be king in marketplaces almost everywhere, in **Canada**, it's actually illegal to pay with too many coins – the Currency Act means you can use a maximum of 25 pennies, 100 nickels, 100 dimes, 40 quarters, 25 ones and 20 twos in any one transaction.

– that's the height of arrogance and can cause huge offense. Touching products or trying clothes on before you buy them is not necessarily allowed either – sometimes a dedicated sample is supplied for people to handle, and in **Japan** women are expected to put on a supplied face mask before trying on clothes to prevent getting make-up on the garments.

As with every encounter, it's important to treat market vendors and retail workers with courtesy and respect – you're never going to get a better deal by being rude, so jerks always lose out in the end. In the **USA**, and also in **Japan**, staff often greet shoppers at the door. In some countries, such as **Korea**, staff will follow you round the store asking all sorts of questions and trying to be helpful – an approach many people find a bit claustrophobic; if this bothers you, politely point out that you are just browsing and make it clear that you'd like to be given some space (although this often won't work, and you basically have to learn to live with it). Conversely, don't expect too much effusive customer service in countries such as **Britain**, **France** and **Italy**, where staff often give the appearance that they couldn't care less whether you make a purchase or not.

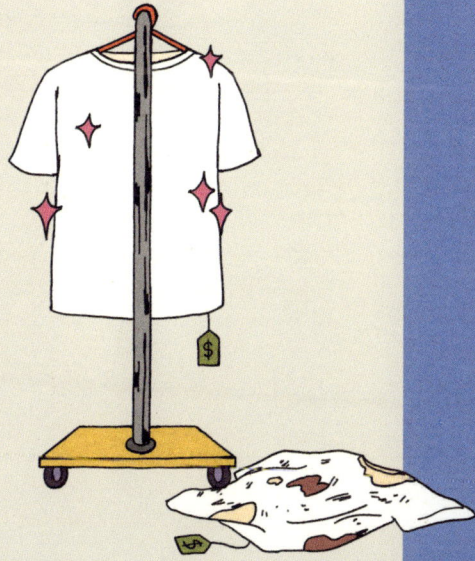

ODE ON A (FAUX) GRECIAN URN

IS IT REALLY BAD IF I BUY THIS RARE ANTIQUITY?

Firstly, is it *really* what the seller purports it to be? Unless you're an expert, it can be very easy to get conned while you're traveling in unfamiliar territory. If something that is supposedly both rare and ancient is being hawked on the side of the street for a price you can casually afford to pay, you need to have a serious think about its authenticity – fake 'antiques' are common the world over.

Shopping at Outdoor Markets

Markets, bazaars and souks are the most exciting places in the world to go shopping. Some – such as the Grand Bazaar in **İstanbul**, **Türkiye**, Chatuchak Weekend Market in **Bangkok**, **Thailand**, and Djemaa El Fna and Medina Souk in **Marrakesh**, **Morocco** – are vibrant, almost overwhelmingly sensational destinations; each is the size of a small town, with myriad labyrinthine laneways full of colorful stalls and stands selling everything you could possibly imagine, and plenty more besides. If you enter these places, you are not leaving empty-handed, so you might just as well accept that. And in between browsing the table-top treasure troves, you can often get a head massage, haircut or a killer wet shave while watching street entertainers woo onlookers out of the corner of your eye.

DO I HAVE TO BRING CASH?

Some of the world's most fascinating markets date back many hundreds of years (Chandni Chowk in **Delhi**, **India** was built in the 17th century by the Mughal Emperor Shah Jahan; Khan Al Khalili in **Cairo**, **Egypt**, has a history stretching back to 1382), and in some ways they feel timeless. Elements of modernity are creeping in, and some vendors can accept electronic and credit-card payments these days, but cash is still very much the preferred currency – so yes, you do need to carry some actual notes. But if you're heading to a hectic part of town or a bustling

TOP TIP
In some Asian countries, including Japan, if you pay cash for an item in a store it is customary to place the money on a plate that the seller will present to you.

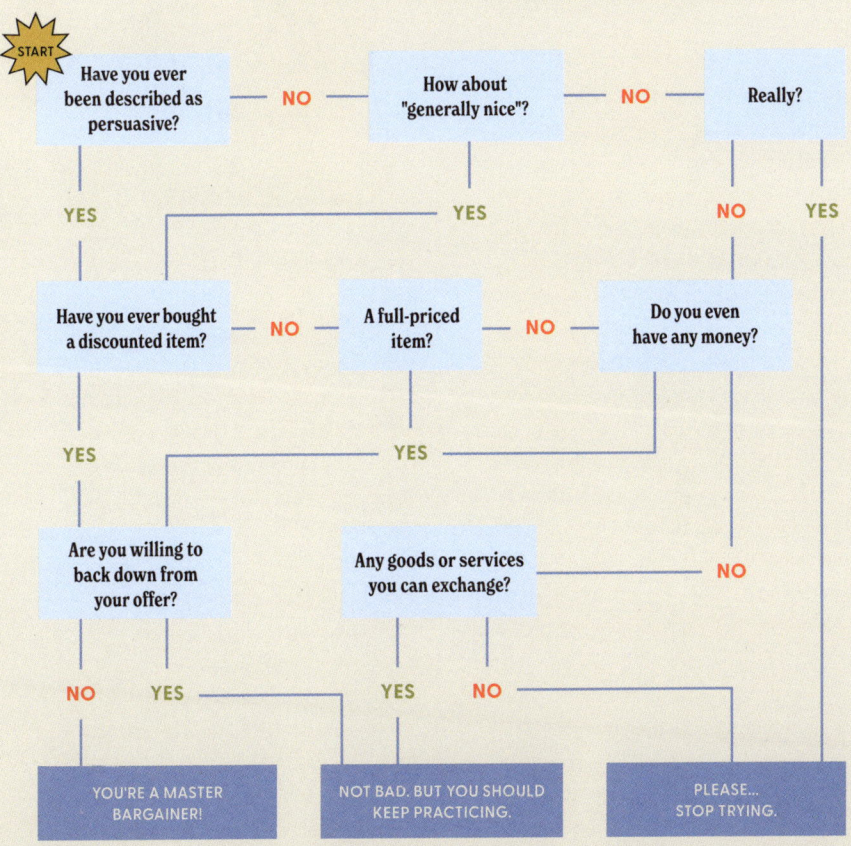

marketplace where there are inevitably pickpockets at work, don't carry large amounts of money (also avoid wearing flashy jewelry and watches, and other indicators of wealth – such trappings won't work in your favor when you're bartering). And make sure to have some smaller denominations too.

HOW AND WHEN TO BARTER

Haggling over the price of items in an outdoor market, bazaar or souk is something many travelers struggle with at first, but it can be a thrilling experience and can become quite addictive. Starting low and negotiating with a seller, making a big deal out of walking away only to be tempted back in by a new lowest offer – it's all part of the game. Here's a few tips for when not to barter too hard.

When items in markets are clearly marked with a price tag: casually asking whether there is a discount for buying three of the same thing (like a T-shirt or tea towel) is fine, and will often pay dividends, but offering a much-reduced

amount for a clearly labeled product is just rude.

In shopping malls full of brand-name stores – you might find a place with a sale on, but generally speaking prices are fixed in these places.

In boutiques and general stores – there are set prices for things in such places the world over (though you might score a discount on damaged goods or food that's fast approaching its expiration date – it's worth asking). You can push as hard as you like when haggling over a plastic souvenir likely mass-produced in **China**, but when purchasing a legitimate local product crafted by someone from carefully sourced materials, pay a fair price. In

TOP TIP

Don't be too serious when bartering, have some fun – market vendors often enjoy a bit of banter. If you have learned a few polite words in the local language, use them.

some cultures, such as in **Japan**, bartering happens far less frequently and much more subtly, within respectful boundaries – take your lead from locals.

Street and market vendors are extremely savvy businesspeople – they have to be, given they likely live much more perilously close to the poverty line than anyone who can afford to buy a book like this. You might walk away from an exchange in Khan Al Khalili in **Cairo**, **Egypt**, the Fundo el Fierro artisan market in **Arequipa**, **Peru**, or the Mutrah Souk in **Muscat**, **Oman**, thinking you've just wrangled the deal of the century, but in all likelihood, the person on the other side of the counter had long ago decided how low they would go, and you probably didn't get anywhere near it. If you really want something, they can smell it. You might think you're scoring a bargain by finding another stand nearby selling the same thing, and playing them off against one other, but they've seen all this before. It's a sport where everyone walks away thinking they're the winner (and that's the best kind of sport).

It's important to always stay respectful, however, no matter how animated the discussions get; don't relentlessly try to screw every last cent out of each exchange. If you really want

WHAT A RUSH!

IS THIS REAL GOLD?

If you're perusing the wares at a proper artisan market like the Old Medina in **Essaouira**, **Morocco**, or looking at glittery bits and bobs in the Gold Souk in **Dubai**, then the stuff is almost certainly the real deal; at a backstreet bazaar in downtown **Delhi**, however, or a flea market in **London**, **Paris** or **New York**, you might want to be a bit more cynical and circumspect. Feel and inspect the product, but for God's sake don't bite it – you'll damage it, and who knows where it has been or who has handled it previously… Often, even in places like Camden Lock Market in **London**, jewelry made with real gold and silver will be sold by weight. The final price is always the most telling thing – if it feels like you got an unbelievable bargain, then you've probably been rolled.

TRAVEL ETIQUETTE TIPS

Don't assume that ju
a country with lower
standards than your
over the price of eve
the height of arroga
huge offense.

t because you're in
socioeconomic living
own, you can barter
y purchase — that's
ce and can cause

AN ALIGNMENT CHART

HOW UNHINGED IS THAT SOUVENIR?

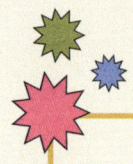

LAWFUL GOOD	NEUTRAL GOOD	CHAOTIC GOOD
BOTTLE OF WINE	**CHOCOLATE OR CANDY**	**THEMED SHOTGLASS**
LAWFUL NEUTRAL	TRUE NEUTRAL	CHAOTIC NEUTRAL
LOCAL CURRENCY	**SNOWGLOBE**	**KEYCHAIN**
LAWFUL EVIL	NEUTRAL EVIL	CHAOTIC EVIL
OFFENSIVE T-SHIRT	**FRIDGE MAGNET**	**FERTILITY DOLL**

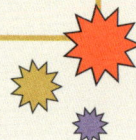

something, then recognize it has a real value and you ought to pay a reasonable amount for it – while you're highly unlikely to get one over on battle-hardened marketplace vendors, in some scenarios you can come out on top, but at what price, really? I have an African chief's chair in the corner of my living room that would probably be my most prized possession from my travels if it wasn't for the chisel-sharp pangs of guilt I feel every time I look at it – because deep down I know that, in the heat of the haggling moment and full of youthful ignorance, I really didn't pay the guy who carved it enough. I often sit on this wooden pew and wish myself back 25 years to the shore of Lake Malawi so I can make amends – it never works, so all I can do is urge you not to make the same mistake.

SHOULD I PAY THE TOURIST PRICE?

In many ways this is an academic question. You don't have much choice other than to pay the 'tourist' price in places where this kind of unofficial tariff is often applied – which happens in markets everywhere, from **Ecuador** to **Egypt** – because, while you might consider yourself a 'traveler', the vendor knows you are, in fact, a tourist. But often there's a sliding scale on such things – sellers are usually experienced and astute people-readers, so if you come across as comparatively rich and a bit arrogant, they'll sting you hard. Act respectfully, but ultimately – unless you're shopping in wealthier regions – you shouldn't resent locals supporting themselves with their wares.

TOP TIP

While it's fine to spot a small defect or blemish and try to negotiate the price down, don't insult the seller – especially if they are also the maker – by insinuating that the product is a virtually worthless piece of garbage and offering next to nothing to take it off their hands.

Shopping for Souvenirs

Even when shopping in locations like **Scotland** and **Ireland**, it can be surprisingly hard to find a keepsake that will remind you of your travels that is actually produced locally – so many items that are presented with some sort of cultural insignia are actually mass-produced in another country. If you want something more authentic, which funnels funds into the local economy, avoid souvenir outlets altogether (and definitely don't wait until you're at the airport). Instead, seek out smaller craft shops, where you can find genuine items that will remind you of your trip – even if they're not wrapped in the flag of the country where you bought them. Consider steering clear of the more stereotypical items – especially if they might seem culturally appropriative – and seek out something a bit more thoughtful. Buying a book from a locally renowned author at a boutique bookshop is a great way to support local culture and take a tangible memory home with you.

It's also really important to avoid items that contribute to destruction of the environment, depletion of the local habitat, or degradation of historical sites. Avoid purchasing anything that contains animal parts, including shells, skin, eggs, bone, feathers and fossils. And don't buy bits of local landmarks, either (you're likely being conned anyway: genuine bricks from the Berlin Wall have long since disappeared, so

TOP TIP
Treat all vendors with the same respect you would expect people to show you – it's not a real battle, you are just shopping for souvenirs, presents and keepsakes, so keep it in perspective.

what you're proudly displaying as a historic relic is just a random piece of rubble that some enterprising soul has spray-painted and put a price tag on).

BUYING ORIGINAL ARTWORKS

One of the best reminders of a special traveling experience – like a honeymoon – is purchasing a piece of original art from a local sculptor or painter. When sourcing such a precious item, it makes it extra special if you can buy directly from the artist, and this also cuts out the risk that an unscrupulous agent or intermediary is charging you a fortune and taking a cut. This is especially important when buying Indigenous art in places like **Central Australia** and

BEFRIENDING THE TSA

WILL THIS KATANA MAKE IT THROUGH CUSTOMS?

Often while traveling, you will come across items that are presented as traditional (or not so traditional) weapons but dressed up as souvenirs for tourists, ranging from Maasai spears in **Kenya** to ceremonial swords in **Bengal** and **Nepal**, to hideous-looking knuckledusters, flick-knives and throwing stars on the streets of **Bangkok**. It's really not a great idea to buy such products, not least because the customs officials waiting to welcome you back home might not be thrilled to see deadly weapons being brought into the country. It's also a form of cultural appropriation that dilutes the importance of cultural or ceremonial objects by making them seem like toys. Admire the weapons of great warriors old and new, but leave the katana swords for the real samurais. It won't seem all that impressive displayed next to your nerf gun at home.

the **Northern Territory**, where both naive tourists and local artists are regularly ripped off. Go to a gallery with a certificate of authenticity (proving they work with local people), or inquire at a visitor information center about the best places to see and buy Indigenous artwork. If you are lucky enough to meet the artist (and this is often possible), treat them with respect and pay a fair price for a piece of art they have invested a large amount of time and channeled many generations of learning and skill into creating.

This isn't the time for hardcore haggling, and while it's worth having a 'highest price you are prepared to pay' in your head, if you're trying to buy something unique that you're unlikely to ever see or get the opportunity to buy again, don't miss out for the sake of a few bucks.

RULES OF THUMB FOR LARGER PURCHASES

If you are considering buying something substantial – either expensive or physically large, or both, like a rug or a sculpture – you need to think hard about the logistics of carrying it around and worrying about it for the rest of your trip. The ideal scenario is picking up such things at the end of your odyssey, but if this isn't possible, it might be worth shipping them home and making sure they comply with customs law. Either way, setting your heart on something fragile is probably a very bad idea.

TOP TIP

As much as it might feel like a game to you, vendors and stallholders are trying to eke out a real living, so don't waste their time or set false expectations if you have no intention of actually buying.

✸ HELPFUL ✸ DOS AND DON'TS

WHEN SHOPPING

DO treat everyone – from market vendors and street sellers to shop staff – with politeness and respect.

DON'T take food or drinks with you into boutique or even standard stores (though it's usually fine to munch your way around marketplaces).

DO carry some cash (including smaller denominations) when perusing markets, souks and bazaars.

DON'T assume you can barter for everything you want to buy.

DO accept that if you break something, you have to buy it – this is a universal law.

DON'T assume you can touch stuff and try on anything you like – just ask first.

DO pay a fair price for pieces of genuine artwork and handmade craft items.

DON'T buy souvenirs made with exotic animals or pieces of local monuments.

DO make sure your souvenirs adhere to local customs laws

DON'T buy large, heavy, or oversized items without a solid plan for how to get them back home.

Conclusion

LOOKING BACK over a long (I hope) life of national and international travel, one thing I am sure you will never, ever regret is having been decent to the people you met during your journeys. You might wish you'd stayed in a particular location for a little bit longer, picked up a special piece of artwork that you've never been able to forget, spotted a wild animal you'd set your heart on seeing, or made it to the top of a peak you were hoping to climb – but while you have puff in your lungs and a passport in your pocket, you can always return to those destinations and try again. What you really can't do is scoot back in time and apologize for treating someone badly, or carelessly causing offense with some dumbass cultural faux pas you could have easily avoided.

You don't need to have **Swiss**-finishing-school-perfect manners, or have swotted up on every element of etiquette in each destination you are planning to visit – there isn't a traveler out there who hasn't dropped a major clanger at some point, and it's all part of the educational experience that travel is uniquely able to deliver. But you do need to learn how to coexist with the people you meet. Especially the locals and your long-suffering hosts, who have to endure endless amounts of visitors shouting loudly at them and waving their arms around, as if that helps complex questions (like 'Where's the bloody

Looking back over a long (I hope) life of national and international travel, one thing I am sure you will never, ever regret is having been decent to the people you met during your journeys.

ketchup?', and 'Why can't I wear my swimsuit in church?') sail smoothly across the linguistic and cultural divide.

I'm sure you started out as the best kind of person anyway, but having since been lured in by vague title promises of content about hiking in the buff, I do hope this book has been proven useful. And perhaps, if you know someone who has tendencies towards being a thoughtless traveler, you could subtly get them a copy. Remember not to give it to them with your left hand, though, and be sure to stare them straight in the eye when you hand it over.

Just maybe, if we collectively encourage everyone we know to spend more time listening to the people they meet while traveling, instead of shouting at them, and to exercise a little empathy once in a while, we might make a microdot of a difference. For my money, it's worth a try, even if I do end up looking like a total jerk.

BON VOYAGE!

Acknowledgments

I WOULD LIKE TO SAY A HUGE THANKS to Becca and Jenni for their endless patience, enormous expertise and excellent editorial judgement and juggling skills. And also Taylor for lending her exceptional design talent to this book.

And I want to thank my wife, Steph, who — very wisely — never lets me hike naked anywhere, let alone in Switzerland, but has put up with myriad mortifying gaffes, faux pas and foot-in-mouth moments during two and a half decades of travelling with me.

Index

A
accommodations 33-49
Airbnb 44-5
animals 18, 76, 109
  photography 105
antiques 117
apologising 67
Argentina
  clothing 103
  drinking 84, 85
  kissing 57
  table manners 81
art galleries 98-9
artworks 95, 99, 127-8
Australia
  sacred sites 108-10
  shaking hands 60
  table manners 80-1
  tipping 40, 88
Austria
  shaking hands 60
  tipping 88

B
Barbados
  clothing 103
bartering 119, 120, 125
B&Bs 42

beer 87
Belgium
  drinking 84, 87
  hand gestures 68
  kissing 57
Bolivia
  drinking 84
Bosnia
  kissing 57
Botswana
  shaking hands 61
bowing 61, 64-5
Brazil
  hand gestures 66-7
  kissing 57
  shaking hands 60
  toilets 47
Bulgaria
  hand gestures 68
buses 24-5, 31

C
Cambodia
  greetings 65
  table manners 78, 81
  tipping 41-2
Canada
  queuing 95

  table manners 78
  tipping 41, 88
Caribbean
  hand gestures 68
  tipping 41
car rental 30
cash 116, 118, 120
cathedrals 100
checking in 36
Chile
  kissing 57
  table manners 80
China
  apologising 67
  bowing 65
  drinking 86
  formal language 61
  queuing 95
  shaking hands 60
  table manners 78, 80
  tipping 41-2
  toilets 47
churches 100
clothing 100, 102-3
Colombia
  kissing 57
conversation 23, 29, 51-69
Croatia
  clothing 102

kissing 57
Czechia
  drinking 87

D
Denmark
  drinking 87
dining 71-89
dos & don'ts
  lodging 49
  public transport 31
  shopping 129
  sightseeing 111
  talking to strangers 69
drinking 72-3, 84-7
  airports 16-17
driving 30

E
eating 71-89
  ethics 76
  public transport 19
Egypt
  drinking 84, 86
  kissing 57
  table manners 78, 80
  toilets 47
endangered animals 76
Estonia
  table manners 81
Ethiopia
  table manners 80-1
Europe
  shaking hands 60
  taxis 28
  tipping 88
eye contact 22-3

F
ferries 25
Fiji
  shaking hands 60
  table manners 81
Finland
  drinking 87
fires 108
flying 16-17
food 71-89
  ethics 76
  public transport 19
foreign languages 54-5
formal language 61
France
  clothing 103
  drinking 84, 85, 86
  hand gestures 68
  jaywalking 29
  photography 104
  shopping 117
  table manners 80-1
  tipping 88

G
Georgia
  drinking 85
Germany
  drinking 86, 87
  kissing 57
  nudity 107
  table manners 81
Ghana
  drinking 86
gifts 85
gold 121
Greece
  hand gestures 66-7
  kissing 57
  table manners 81

toilets 47
greetings 51-69

H
haggling 119, 120, 125
hand gestures 30, 66-8
hiking 106-7
hitchhiking 30
Hong Kong
  table manners 80
hostels 46-8
hotels 36-41
Hungary
  clothing 103
  drinking 87
  kissing 57

I
Iceland
  taxis 28
  tipping 28, 40
India
  greetings 65
  hand gestures 68
  queuing 95
  table manners 78, 81
  tipping 88
  toilets 47
Indigenous art 127-8
Indigenous peoples 109-10
Indonesia
  shaking hands 60
  tipping 41-2
Iran
  drinking 85
  hand gestures 67
Ireland
  drinking 84, 85, 86, 87
  jaywalking 29

taxis 28
tipping 28, 40, 88
Israel
queuing 95
Italy
clothing 102
drinking 84, 86
hand gestures 67-8
kissing 57
photography 104
queuing 95
shopping 117
table manners 80-1

J

Jamaica
clothing 103
Japan
apologising 67
bowing 61, 64-5
drinking 84, 86, 87
haggling 121
jaywalking 29
pregnancy 23
public transport 21
queuing 94
shoes 45
shopping 116
table manners 78, 80-1
taxis 28
tipping 28, 41, 88
toilets 46

K

Kazakhstan
drinking 85
Kenya
drinking 86
shaking hands 61-2

table manners 78, 81
kissing 56-9

L

language 54-5, 61
Laos
greetings 65
left hand use 60
LGBTIQ+ travellers 41
lining up 94-5, 101
lodging 33-49
luggage 16, 18, 20

M

Macedonia
kissing 57
Malaysia
table manners 78
tipping 41-2
Maldives
clothing 102
markets 118-21
meeting people 23, 29, 51-69
menus 75-6
Mexico
shaking hands 60
table manners 80-1

Middle East
hand gestures 66
shaking hands 60
table manners 78
Montenegro
kissing 57
Morocco
shaking hands 60
table manners 78
mosques 100
Mozambique
shaking hands 60
museums 98-9

N

Nepal
greetings 65
Netherlands
clothing 103
kissing 57
tipping 88
**New Zealand/
Aotearoa**
shaking hands 60
tipping 40, 88

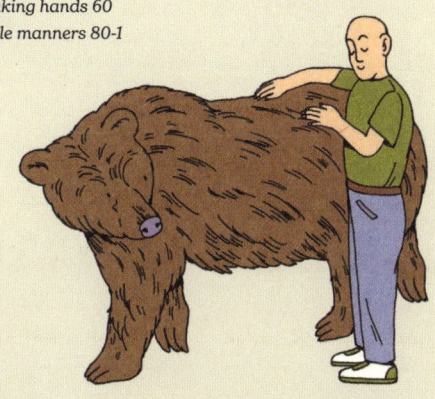

Nigeria
  clothing 103
  nudity *106, 107*

O
older people *21, 55*
Oman
  clothing 103
  ordering *75-6, 81*
  outdoor activities *106-10*

P
packing *20*
Pakistan
  hand gestures 68
  personal space *68*
Peru
  kissing 57
Philippines
  drinking 86
  hand gestures 67
  kissing 57
  older people 55
  table manners 78
  tipping 41-2

photography *99, 104-5*
planes *16-17, 31*
Poland
  clothing 103
  drinking 86
politics *55*
Portugal
  drinking 86
  table manners 80-1
public land *106*
public transportation *13-31*
punctuality *77*

Q
queuing *94-5, 101*

R
reclining seats *17-18*
religious sites *100*
reservations *77*
  hotels 36
Romania
  kissing 57
room service *37*
Russia
  drinking 85, 87
  hand gestures 67
  kissing 57

shaking hands 60
table manners 78

S
same-sex travellers *41*
Saudi Arabia
  clothing 103
Scandinavia
  drinking 86
  right to roam 106
  taxis 28
  tipping 28, 40, 88
Scotland
  clothing 103
  right to roam 106
selfies *104-5*
Serbia
  drinking 86
  kissing 57
shaking hands
  59-61
shoes *45*
shopping *113-29*
shrines *100*
sightseeing *91-111*
sign language *66-8*
Singapore
  hand gestures 67
  jaywalking 29
  table manners 81
  taxis 28
  tipping 28, 41-2
  toilets 47
Slovenia
  kissing 57
South America
  tipping 41, 88
South Korea
  bowing 61, 64-5
  drinking 84, 86

138

jaywalking 29
pregnancy 23
shaking hands 60
shopping 116-17
table manners 78, 80-1
taxis 28
tipping 28, 88
souvenirs 124, 126-8
Spain
 clothing 102
 drinking 86
 hand gestures 67-8
 kissing 57
 public transport 18
Sri Lanka
 greetings 65
 photography 105
 tipping 88
statues 95, 99
stealing 37, 84, 108
subway 21-3
swimwear 102-3
Switzerland
 kissing 57
 nudity 107
 toilets 47

T

table manners 78, 80-3
talking to strangers 23, 29, 51-69
Tanzania
 shaking hands 61-2
taxis 28-9
temples 100
Thailand
 drinking 86
 greetings 65
 personal space 56
 queuing 95

table manners 78, 80
tipping 41-2, 88
tipping 88
 hotels 40-1
toasting 86, 87
toilets 46, 47, 96-7
tour buses 25
tourist prices 125
trains 18-19, 31
Trinidad & Tobago
 clothing 103
Tunisia
 hand gestures 66, 68
Türkiye
 clothing 103
 hand gestures 66
 shaking hands 60

U

UK
 drinking 84, 87
 hand gestures 67
 pregnancy 23
 queuing 94
 shaking hands 60
 shopping 117
 table manners 80-1
 taxis 28
 tipping 28, 40, 88
unfamiliar foods 74, 79
USA
 clothing 102-3
 hand gestures 66
 Indigenous sites 110
 jaywalking 29
 photography 104
 queuing 94
 shopping 116
 table manners 80
 tipping 40, 88

V

Venezuela
 kissing 57
Vietnam
 hand gestures 68-9
 table manners 81
 tipping 41-2

W

weapons 127
wine 85

Z

Zambia
 clothing 103
Zimbabwe
 clothing 103
 shaking hands 60

Don't Hike Naked in Switzerland
April 2026
Published by Lonely Planet Global Limited
CRN: 554153
ISBN: 9781837587674
© Lonely Planet
10 9 8 7 6 5 4 3 2 1
Printed in Malaysia

Publisher & VP, Print Piers Pickard
Publisher, Gift & Illustrated Becca Hunt
Project Editor Jenni Zellner
Creative Direction Emily Dubin
Art Direction and Design Taylor Miles Hopkins
Print Production Nigel Longuet
Copyeditor Polly Thomas
Proofreader Nick Mee
Author Patrick Kinsella
Illustrator Kaitlin Brito

All rights reserved. No part of this publication may be reproduced, stored in a retrieval system or transmitted in any form by any means, electronic, mechanical, photocopying, recording or otherwise except brief extracts for the purpose of review, without the written permission of the publisher. Lonely Planet and the Lonely Planet logo are trademarks of Lonely Planet and are registered in the US Patent and Trademark Office and in other countries.

Although the author and Lonely Planet have taken all reasonable care in preparing this book, we make no warranty about the accuracy or completeness of its content and, to the maximum extent permitted, disclaim all liability from its use.

STAY IN TOUCH lonelyplanet.com/contact

Lonely Planet Global Limited
Digital Depot, Roe Lane (off Thomas St),
Digital Hub, Dublin 8,
D08 TCV4
Ireland

Paper in this book is certified against the Forest Stewardship Council™ standards. FSC™ promotes environmentally responsible, socially beneficial and economically viable management of the world's forests.